Key Concepts in
Tourism Research

The SAGE Key Concepts series provides students with accessible and authoritative knowledge of the essential topics in a variety of disciplines. Cross-referenced throughout, the format encourages critical evaluation through understanding. Written by experienced and respected academics, the books are indispensable study aids and guides to comprehension.

DAVID BOTTERILL &
VINCENT PLATENKAMP

Key Concepts in
Tourism Research

Los Angeles | London | New Delhi
Singapore | Washington DC

David Botterill and Vincent Platenkamp © 2012

First published 2012

SAGE Publications Ltd
1 Oliver's Yard
55 City Road
London EC1Y 1SP

SAGE Publications Inc.
2455 Teller Road
Thousand Oaks, California 91320

SAGE Publications India Pvt Ltd
B 1/I 1 Mohan Cooperative Industrial Area
Mathura Road
New Delhi 110 044

SAGE Publications Asia-Pacific Pte Ltd
3 Church Street
#10-04 Samsung Hub
Singapore 049483

Library of Congress Control Number: 2011932179

British Library Cataloguing in Publication data

A catalogue record for this book is available from the British Library

ISBN 978-1-84860-174-1
ISBN 978-1-84860-175-8 (pbk)

Typeset by C&M Digitals (P) Ltd, Chennai, India
Printed in India at Replika Press Pvt Ltd
Printed on paper from sustainable resources

Contents

key concepts in
tourism research

About the Authors

David Botterill is a freelance academic and higher education consultant, Visiting Research Fellow at the Centre for Tourism at the University of Westminster and Professor Emeritus in the Welsh Centre for Tourism Research, University of Wales Institute Cardiff. He is also an Associate Director for the Higher Education Academy Network for Hospitality, Leisure, Sport and Tourism and an Associate of the NHTV University of Applied Sciences Breda. David studied at Surrey and Loughborough universities in the 1970s and gained industrial experience in the private and government sectors of the hotel and leisure industries prior to completing a PhD at Texas A & M University in 1987. He returned to the UK to lecture in tourism studies and moved to Cardiff in 1993. He has extensive UK experience of research leadership in university education, most recently as Director of Research in the Cardiff School of Management (1999–2007) at the University of Wales Institute Cardiff. He was promoted to a personal chair of the University of Wales in 2003. He has taken a particular interest in the global development of doctoral level tourism studies as supervisor and external examiner to candidates in the UK and mainland Europe. He is an author and reviewer for several publishing houses and external assessor of research quality for universities and research bodies. Over the past 25 years he has secured and directed consultancy projects for: universities; the Higher Education Academy; the tourism industry; European, national and local governments; and NGOs. He has published extensively in the tourism and leisure studies journals and together with Trevor Jones of Cardiff University recently published an edited book on Tourism and Crime: *Key Issues* for Goodfellow Publishers (2010). In 2011 David was a visiting scholar at The Cairns Institute, James Cook University.

Vincent Platenkamp is Associate Professor at the Centre for Cross-Cultural Understanding at the NHTV University of Applied Sciences Breda, Netherlands. Vincent was educated in Belgium and the Netherlands graduating from the University of Amsterdam with masters degrees in sociology and

about the authors

philosophy, both with Cum Laude honours. From 1977 to 1980 he was a teaching assistant in the philosophy of science and in methodology at the University of Amsterdam and from 1981 to 1989 he worked in The Hague at Stichting SOSA, Haarlem University of Applied Science providing part-time education opportunities in human resource management and labour relations. Vincent joined the NHTV in 1988 and has been extensively involved in HRM, TQM and Cross-Cultural Studies projects in the Netherlands, Portugal, Indonesia, Thailand, Hungary, Poland, Cuba, Curacao and Bulgaria. For 20 years he has been strongly involved in the development of international higher education in tourism and in 2005 was awarded a PhD from Wageningen University for his study of the International Classroom of Tourism Studies. Vincent publishes in both philosophy and tourism studies journals in the Dutch, French and English languages.

David Botterill and Vincent Platenkamp

The underlying premise in our approach to this book is that tourism research is predominately social research and we should therefore look to the social sciences for its anchor points. By placing tourism research within the social sciences we open up to a vast array of philosophical positions, academic disciplines, bodies of theory and methods. The *SAGE Encyclopaedia of Social Science Research Methods*, for example, includes over 1000 entries in three volumes and the task of selecting 33 key concepts for this book has proved a nerve-wracking challenge for us. Our final selections, and omissions, will probably be a point of contention among our readers.

The starting points for our selections are our two different intellectual frames of reference both of which are located within a Western philosophical tradition. David's engagement with tourism research has been conducted within the English-language canon of Anglo-American social science. Vincent's intellectual world is what David might call continental or European, transacted in the French and German languages and, of course, his native Dutch. We have tried to reflect both frames of reference in our choices of key concepts and hope that this results in a richness that is reflected in our list of key concepts and in the text of this book. The global reach of tourism and the concomitant spread of tourism scholarship to all parts of the world highlights our Western biases. We acknowledge that different philosophical influences from the East and the South will, over time, have a greater influence over tourism scholarship than we have been able to reflect in this edition of *Key Concepts in Tourism Research*.

We justify our choice of key concepts in two ways. For the most part, we are able to show how each of the key concepts we have selected has been applied in tourism research through a review of its application to tourism studies. Consequentially, we can claim that they are key concepts within tourism research practice. But there is another sense in which we think our list is 'key', not just as a reflection of current practice but also as a progressive influence on the future of tourism research.

Through this book our intention is to ground tourism research practice more directly in the debates in the philosophies, theories and methods of the social sciences. As this book has progressed it has become increasingly clear to us that the emergence of tourism research in the 1960s positioned it in the social sciences at a particular juncture. What we have tried to do in our selections is to show how current practice in tourism research is informed by ideas that have been rethought through over many decades, and in some cases centuries, of intellectual endeavour.

We call this work the 'underlabouring' of tourism research. We think that our concepts are key because they connect tourism research to the still contentious claims of social science as a legitimate contributor to knowledge. Our intention here is that when reading our book tourism researchers at all levels and in all contexts will be encouraged to engage with, and contribute to, these debates. This, we think, would be a progressive move within tourism research that would help to stabilise its place in the social sciences and add maturity to any claims made about tourism knowledge.

How to Use This Book

So the time has come to choose what, and how, you are going to research the phenomenon of tourism for your thesis or dissertation. Hopefully, you will have taken courses or modules in research methods and will have practised the skills you need in order to undertake your research but you cannot, any longer, put off the choice of topic and the way you are going to investigate it. There are a bewildering variety of topics in tourism and almost as many ways of researching them, so we sympathise with your plight. The most useful general advice that we can give you at this point in your studies is to make sure you choose a topic that really interests you because it has to keep you intrigued for several months to come. We also think it is important to think about how your own strengths map against the particular skills needed for the different approaches that are available to you.

Our experiences of supervision tell us that the answers that you come up with to these two questions are not formulated as quickly as most students would like. The answers also do not arrive neatly packaged into product 'strap lines' or media 'sound bites'. It takes time for them to emerge and, more often than not, in parallel rather than one before the other. We have very often encountered students who are floundering in their attempts to come to answers for either one or both of these questions and have wondered what to say or where to send students for inspiration. We have tried asking pertinent questions to extract topics of interest or directed our students to the research journals but these have not always proved to be successful interventions, not least because they can sometimes undermine confidence. At this stage in the research process we have also found that the many excellent guides on how to do research are not what is needed, as they cannot provide that 'spark' that gets you started on a research journey.

This moment is sometimes an awkward silence in early supervisory meetings. In order to fill the silence the temptation is to risk boring our students with our own research, not always very successfully we will admit. That is not to say that we, or many of your supervisors, do not

how to use this book

3

recognise the responsibility to direct students but because we think that research output, at any level, should be an expression of you and not your supervisor. After all, supervisors are not awarded the degree, students are!

So we have written this book to help you come to those answers about your research projects. Our book follows the model of all Key Concept books in the series and is published as an extended glossary of terms that will provide a useful reference point for students embarking on explorations in tourism research. Sometimes the reactions of our students to the language of the social sciences is often hostile. They complain of a lack of consistency in the use of terms and are bewildered by the sometimes contradictory accounts of the same concept. In response, the entries in this book have been written to limit any potential confusion but, at the same time, not to shy away from the sometimes uncomfortably discursive nature of the philosophy of the social sciences.

For each key concept we provide a definition and an initial guide on its potential relevance to your research project. The relevance section draws upon the many such conversations we have had with students over the years. Then, the key concept has been applied to a range of different topics, with examples drawn from the tourism research journals. Remember, these examples show you how other researchers, some of them students, have answered those two questions of 'what' and 'how'. This is supplemented by an elaboration of the main ideas and techniques associated with each key concept.

Having done our best to simplify the concept, it is unravelled a little. First, we invite you to consider the historical development, philosophical pretext and principal claims that surround the concept. Finally, we provide a short critique of the concept, because in our experience some students sometimes become transfixed by the concept. Having got to grips with its complexities they then treat it as something fixed – a foundational entity – forgetting the all important discursive tendency to critique and argument that permeates the social sciences. A full set of references is provided for follow-up reading. For example, maybe your curiosity in the key concept might have been sparked by a particular article from the tourism journals or you may want to know more about how the generic concept developed or can be applied. To account for both of these eventualities we separate our references into generic and tourism specific listings.

If you really are at the very beginning of finding those answers to the 'what' and 'how' questions then you might like to read this book by just dipping into two or three key concepts at a sitting. If you choose this way of using the book then we have also indicated some possible connections between the key concepts in the text by capitalising them and listing them, under a separate heading 'CROSS REFERENCES', setting up an order in which to read other key concepts from the book.

However, encouraged by reviewers of our draft manuscript to cluster the concepts in some way we propose another, more structured, way in which you might read this book. We think everyone should start by reading the entries on Empiricism and Ethical Practice because these are the bedrock of your research activities. Next, our reading of the tourism research literature indicates that one way of categorising research output is in three broad topic categories: experiences, places and organisations. What we suggest, then, is that it is possible to structure your reading of the entries in this book around each of these broad categories.

EXPERIENCES

Let us assume that you have tentatively decided to study the 'experiences' associated with tourism. These might be tourists' or employees' experiences or they may be the experiences of those living in communities who receive tourists. If you have settled on this category of topic for your research then we suggest you should read the following as a set of key concepts: Ethnomethodology, Hermeneutics, Interview/Focus Group, Narrative, Phenomenology, Repertory Grid, Survey, Symbolic Interactionism.

PLACES

If you prefer to study tourism places we suggest the following set of key concepts: Case Study, Content Analysis, Document Analysis, Interview/Focus Group.

If the topic of your research concerns the policies and practices of organisations here is our list of key concepts that might be particularly helpful: Action Research, Case Study, Delphi Method, Document Analysis, Evaluation Research, Grounded Theory.

Now let us take another potential starting point for organising your reading of this book. You know roughly what your topic is but you cannot decide on how to research it. If this is where you are in your thinking then dip into this set of key concepts: Autoethnography, Content Analysis, Delphi Method, Document Analysis, Experiment, Ethnomethodology, Interview/Focus Group, Narrative, Repertory Grid, Survey, Visual Methods. Conversely, your supervisor might be pushing you to set your research ideas into a particular theoretical frame. A favoured criticism by supervisors of what might be called 'superficial' research proposals is that they lack analytical depth. If this is the feedback you've been getting, then the following set of key concepts might just settle your mind and enable you to demonstrate more depth of analysis in your study: Critical Theory, Feminism, Figurationalism, Grounded Theory, Post-colonialism, Postmodernism, Symbolic Interactionism.

Our last suggestion for grouping the key concepts as a set of readings explores a central thrust of our book. As we argue in our Introduction, we think that it is important for anyone doing tourism research to recognise that they are in some small way working towards the production of new knowledge. This inevitably means that tourism researchers at all levels should engage, at an appropriate level, with the philosophy of science and the ever present debate over the contribution of the social sciences to knowledge. So we begin this group of key concepts with what many would consider the most important contemporary debate in the philosophy of science, that between Popper and Kuhn with the suggestion to read Deduction and Paradigm. To complete this, albeit selective, exploration of the philosophy of (social) science we would add the key concepts of Constructionism, Epistemology, Positivism and Realism.

In order to develop greater sophistication in your thinking, then it is time to confront the competing claims of different schools of thought in the social sciences. This can be done by reading the following key concepts as a set: Critical Realism, Critical Theory, Experiment, Hermeneutics, Modelling, Phenomenology, Positivism. You may have heard the term 'Interpretivism' used alongside the key concepts we have included in the book. We considered a separate entry for this topic but for those students wanting a better understanding of Interpretivism we decided that we should instead recommend reading our key concepts entries for Constructionism, Hermeneutics and Phenomenology.

We can only now wish you luck in your studies and hope that *Key Concepts in Tourism Research* is a book that you will remember fondly long after your research project is complete and that you will recommend it to your fellow students, your tutors and even your libraries. No doubt we will get candid feedback from our own students, but if you have something to tell us that would improve the book, then please get in touch with us through our publisher.

NOTE TO FELLOW SUPERVISORS/TUTORS

In the processes of designing a research project there are times when both students and their supervisors might turn to this book in order to refresh their understandings of a concept or to quickly locate examples from the tourism literature that may provide comparator studies.

Reading about a single concept as a starting point for discussion in supervision and deciding if further reading is warranted is one use for the book. However, we hope that tutors will find ways of incorporating the book into research methods teaching in tourism. Although the concepts are ordered alphabetically, they might, for teaching purposes, be organised into groups of concepts and we have indicated some possible combinations above. Individually, or in small groups, students might be encouraged to take a group of key concepts, follow up on the examples of tourism research and attempt to synthesise this material for seminar discussion or as a written assignment. They might be challenged to produce a research proposal following a particular research emphasis, or to select a research topic and design two or more studies of contrasting types.

Finally, a note on our selections of key concepts and on omissions. The choices we have made are driven by our judgments of what we think are the key concepts in tourism research at this point in time. An explanation of why we have not included a separate section on Interpretivism is given above, however, we would certainly acknowledge its recent importance in tourism scholarship. We considered the inclusion of Post-structuralism but preferred, at this stage, to treat it within the key concepts on Epistemology and Postmodernism and to include Post-structuralist argument within various sections that critique other key concepts. Just like the reviewers of the draft manuscript it is likely that, if you were writing this book, you would have included others and omitted some of our selections. Should you have particularly strong views about this we hope you will tell us as, in the event that we get the chance to revise this book in a second edition, we would always want to improve and refine it.

Definition Action Research engages the researcher with participants in cycles of action and reflection to address issues of practical and pressing importance in their lives. It is often visualised as a circular process of planning, action and fact finding about the results of the action.

RELEVANCE

Two factors must be in place to make Action Research a viable approach. First, there must be a commitment to achieving change in a situation or organisation and second, you will need easy access to your research setting, whether it is a tourism destination or commercial or not-for-profit enterprise. To be effective, Action Research demands that you spend time in the research setting to work through one or more action cycles. If you are already involved in a tourism organisation in a voluntary or paid capacity, then you are in a great starting position provided you have the support of the organisation's leadership. Periods of workplace experience can also be turned into Action Research projects but you must discuss this with your employer or supervisor and if there is no commitment to make changes then you will need to reformulate your research strategy, perhaps by choosing another of our key concepts such as Case Study, Ethnomethodology or Grounded Theory.

APPLICATION

Given the origins of Action Research as emerging from within the study of organisations, it is likely that contemporary examples do not always reach the public domain and are documented only as internal reports. This may be a reason for the low numbers of published studies found in the literature. There are sufficient though to illustrate the two orientations of Action Research – the pragmatic and the critical/participatory.

Four studies demonstrate the pragmatic orientation described in more detail in the section on 'historical development' below. Taylor and Taylor (2008) use an Action Research approach in devising new methods for ensuring food safety in the hospitality industry. Hastings et al. (2006) report how Action Research was employed in concert with Case Study research to effect change in the marketing practices of a small-scale tourist attractions consortia in Mid Wales. Hastings undertook her study as part of a Knowledge Transfer Partnership (KTP) between a university and a commercial partner. The aim was to create and manage a new tourism attractions consortia – Dyvi Valley Days – involving four tourist attractions in Mid Wales. Multiple case studies of tourism consortia fed into three cycles of action research. The action research was undertaken over a two-year period and involved learning from nine case study consortia. First-, second- and third-person narratives were used to develop a model of best practice in tourism consortia marketing. A checklist in the form of a series of questions that can be used by consortia to evaluate progress and overcome difficulties was produced and tested on practitioners.

Action Research offers a useful framework for conducting research during a period of consultancy and Sofield's (2007) work on the economy of the Greater Mekong region of China is a good example. Our final example is of a specific derivative of Action Research: appreciative inquiry. Raymond and Hall (2008) demonstrate the potential of appreciative inquiry through the study of good practice in volunteer tourism.

Examples of critical or participatory action research include studies into sustainable tourism in Eastern Indonesia (Cole, 2006) and community participation in planning for tourism in the Arctic regions of Canada (Stewart et al., 2008). In both of these articles the researchers demonstrate their commitment to the empowerment of indigenous communities to better benefit from tourism development. Community participation in planning for tourism is also the rationale for the use of Action Research in Naples although emancipation is not explicit in the rationale of the research (Arcidiacono and Procentese, 2005). This is also the case in an article on livelihood capacity building through an ecotourism community knowledge exchange project in the Suid Bokkeveld region of South Africa (Oettlé et al., 2004).

HISTORICAL DEVELOPMENT

Action Research emerged from the ideas of Kurt Lewin who created it as a process that would allow greater employee involvement in the workplace. Lewin described Action Research 'as a way of generating knowledge about a social system while, at the same time, attempting to change it' (Lewin as quoted in Hart and Bond, 1995: 13). As a social scientist working in the USA in the 1930s and 1940s, Lewin was influenced strongly (and negatively) by the adoption of positivism in social science and (positively) by the ideas of Dewey, James and Pierce, three philosophers in the American school of pragmatism. Lewin's work inspired social researchers who were looking for an alternative to positivism that also incorporated the truth notion of 'practical adequacy' contained within pragmatism. Action Research reached a peak in its first phase of influence in the early 1950s.

Following a gradual decline, Action Research began its second phase of popularity when, in the 1970s, critically oriented social researchers recognised the potential of Action Research as a vehicle for the emancipation of underprivileged groups. During these developments, Action Research shifted from its pragmatic purpose to a more critical approach intent on unveiling dominant ideologies and coercive structures. The rebirth of Action Research was strongly influenced by intellectuals from Latin America, particularly Paulo Freire, and Europe, in the form of contributions to social theory from Jürgen Habermas and Michel Foucault. In the 1990s, Lewin's earlier pragmatist point of departure was recaptured in a new burst of enthusiasm for Action Research, particularly in management studies, as a part of a wider movement to democratise institutions and workplace organisations.

The debate about orientations in Action Research can also be seen as part of the challenge to the power of 'scientific experts' in society. From a critical orientation, Action Research becomes part of broader political agendas, for example, in relation to emancipating previously silent voices in debates about the environment, human rights and development. From a pragmatic orientation, Action Research is seen as contributing to, and the opening up of, the governance of institutions to a wider range of stakeholder groups and influences. This is evident in the higher status given to the knowledge of practitioners and consumers as well as in the promotion of experimental and interactive learning. These two, arguably divergent, strands in Action Research have further developed particular action research methodologies and are steering an internal critique within the action research community (see for example McNiff and Whitehead, 2006 in respect of education).

DESCRIPTION

The central idea that unifies action researchers is that it is a research approach that provides opportunity for participative and change-oriented initiatives. What separates the pragmatic and critical methodologies begins with the position of the researcher within the project. Does s/he engage with practioners to gather their inputs yet exclude them from analysis and theory building activities, or is the researcher a co-participant along with other co-participants who jointly interpret, verify and disseminate the outcomes of the research? The distinctions between the methodologies are subtle but very real and Johansson and Lindhult (2008) detail them in terms of the dimensions of: purpose, action focus, orientation to power, research focus, development focus, and dialogue type.

Pragmatic orientation

Here the purpose is adaptation to a situation and incremental change, the action is experimentation and the research focus is dialogue and experiential learning. Although democratic dialogue is stressed, its realisation is adjusted to the practical requirements of getting the change process started. Consensus building is contained with existing structures of power. Methods such as dialogue conferences and the creation of dialogue spaces wherein the researcher takes on a 'Publican' role (Linhuld as cited in Johansson and Lindhult, 2008: 104) encourage consensus and conflict avoidance. 'Deep Slice' project groups, where individuals from different parts and levels of one or more organisations are tasked with the generation of concrete projects, can provide the start point for Action Research cycles.

Critical orientation

Emancipation is the explicit purpose and this is achieved through the methods of participatory enquiry (Reason and Bradbury, 2008). Dispute and argument are welcomed as constructive parts of the discovery of suppressive power structures. Periods of critical reflection and intervention by the researcher promote consciousness raising within the group so that it may struggle against and be liberated from these powers. The research and development focus is based on human values and far-reaching transformation.

The methods are designed to promote openness to others, for example, in the use of first-, second- and third-person inquiry. Each of these represents a different audience for the research. First-person research incorporates the personal voice of the research in first-person accounts of the research process. Here the emphasis is to foster an inquiring approach to one's own life. First- and second-person inquiry methods are essential to demonstrate a commitment to researcher reflexivity and emphasise the situatedness of the researcher typically found in a critical Action Research orientation.

The practice of researching in a social setting is fully acknowledged in second-person inquiry through the creation of a community of inquiry. Third-person inquiry equates to the more orthodox outcomes of research that attempts to summarise major findings and involves wide dissemination.

POTENTIAL CRITICISM

Action Research has come in for criticism on a number of counts: it invites a values-based approach; it produces only context-specific knowledge; it fails tests of objectivity; and tests of research quality. These criticisms are driven by research approaches in the social sciences that emulate the positivist and post-positivist stances of the natural sciences. The notion of proper research is of an external observer gathering data on a phenomenon through tried and tested methods. Attempts are made to isolate the research object, to effect closure around the phenomenon of interest, even in the open systems of the social world. Analysis seeks to test for patterns of relationships that are constant in order to formulate theories about, and ultimately laws that predict, the social world.

These tenets of 'good' social science are to a greater or lesser extent perceived to be compromised by action researchers. For example, in Hastings' work she entered the research with a shared commitment to embrace the values of positive change to affect improved performance in the tourism business consortium, in order to contribute to improved livelihoods for the workforce and the economy of Mid Wales, and to improve the visitor experience for tourists. She became immersed in the host business and adopted projects that were integral to the operations of the organisations she was researching thereby blurring the boundaries between researcher and employee. Her approach was to look outward to discover best practice through the case study method, rather than focus inwards on her own organisation. She embraced an open systems approach to research. Reflections on the impacts of experimentation were used as a platform for further action, rather than necessarily contributing to theory building. Her model building was first validated by practioners before exposure to the wider tourism research community.

The debate between social scientists and action researchers has been addressed by a number of researchers in the field of education (see for example Whitehead and McNiff, 2006) and tourism researchers are encouraged to refer to these debates in order to clarify their own thinking about Action Research.

CROSS REFERENCES

Critical Theory, Evaluation Research.

FURTHER READING

Generic

Hart, E. and Bond, M. (1995) *Action Research for Health and Social Care: A Guide to Practice*. Buckingham: Open University Press.

Johansson, A.W. and Lindhult, E. (2008) Emancipation or workability? Critical versus pragmatic scientific orientation in action research, *Action Research*, 6 (1): 95–115.

Kemmis, S. and McTaggart, R. (2000) Participatory action research, in N.K. Denzin and Y.S. Lincoln (eds), *Handbook of Qualitative Research*, 2nd edn. London: Sage. pp. 567–605.

McNiff, J. and Whitehead, J. (2006) *All You Need to Know About Action Research*. London: Sage.

Reason, P. and Bradbury, H. (eds) (2008) *The SAGE Handbook of Action Research Participative Inquiry and Practice*, 2nd edn. London: Sage.

Whitehead, J. and McNiff, J. (2006) *Action Research Living Theory*. London: Sage.

Tourism specific

Arcidiacono, C. and Procentese, F. (2005) Distinctiveness and sense of community in the historical center of Naples: a piece of participatory research, *Journal of Community Psychology*, 33 (6): 631–8.

Cole, S. (2006) Information and empowerment: the keys to achieving sustainable tourism, *Journal of Sustainable Tourism*, 14 (6): 629–44.

Hastings, E., Jones, E. and Botterill, D. (2005) Tourism marketing consortia best practice: dynamic modelling using action research. Proceedings of Cutting Edge Research in Tourism – New Directions, Challenges and Applications, Surrey University, 6–9 June.

Oettlé, N., Arendse, A., Koelle, B. and Van Der Poll, A. (2004) Community exchange and training in Suid Bokkeveld: a UNCCD pilot project to enhance livelihoods and natural resource management, *Environmental Monitoring and Assessment*, 99 (1–3): 115–25.

key concepts in
tourism research

Raymond, E.M. and Hall, C.M. (2008) The potential for appreciative inquiry in tourism research, *Current Issues in Tourism*, 11 (3): 281–92.

Sofield, T.H.B. (2007) The role of tourism in transition economies of the Greater Mekong sub-region, in J. Cochrane (ed.), *Asian Tourism: Growth and Change*. London: Elsevier. pp. 39–53.

Stewart, E.J., Jacobsen, D. and Draper, D. (2008) Public participation geographic information systems (PPGIS): challenges of implementation in Churchill, Manitoba, *Canadian Geographer*, 52 (3): 351–66.

Taylor, E. and Taylor, J. (2008) A new method of HACCP for hospitality: from concept to project, *International Journal of Contemporary Hospitality Management*, 20 (5): 524–41.

Autoethnography

Definition Autoethnography is a research approach in which the researcher uses her or his own emotions, thoughts and experiences to explore aspects of her or his subculture or culture.

RELEVANCE

Events on a study field trip or personal experiences of travel and tourism as a tourist or as an employee can all be excellent starting points for Autoethnographic research projects but, and it is a very big 'BUT', you need to ask yourself some important questions and answer them very honestly before you embark on a study such as this. Are you prepared to write yourself into your research? Autoethnography requires you to make public the very personal responses and reactions to the situations you write about. Do you really want to share these with your supervisors and examiners? Would you be overwhelmed with embarrassment if you were to speak about these feelings in conversations with your mentors or examiners? Are you ready for the kind of introspective, self analysis that Autoethnography requires? The events taken from your life are just starting points for extensive periods of reflection and analysis. Are you prepared to put the time into thinking about your reactions to events from your life, or are you too busy charging into the next set of events? Are you comfortable with creative writing? If you can write well and are confident of your storytelling talents, then they will stand you in good stead but these are not learned 'on the job' and you will need to have demonstrated your ability, in poetry or creative writing perhaps, before you start on an Autoethnographic project. Lastly, is your supervisor supportive of Autoethnography? This is most important as Autoethnography requires the abandonment of many of the accepted norms of social research. If your supervisor says 'auto ... what?', then our advice would be to turn to another of our key concepts for inspiration or seek to change your supervisor!

APPLICATION

Sikes (2006), Botterill (2003) and Noy (2007a; 2007b) nicely demonstrate the heterogeneity of subject and style of writing found in autoethnographic work in tourism. Noy's (2007b) study comes closest to the blurring of the boundaries between the humanities and social science. His is a poetic response to a family trip to Eilat.

> Through interpreting qualitative material, in the form of a poem I wrote in 1994 about a short familial excursion to an Israeli seaside resort city (Eilat), the research seeks to sensitively describe the intricacies of travel experience. The research explores the advantages of the autoethnographic method of inquiry, and discusses tourism-related emotions and memories in the context of performance and representation. (Noy, 2007b: 141).

Botterill (2003) reflects on his research career through a narrative account of a journey into tourism research that interweaves the personal, professional and intellectual. The article is structured around three questions that provide the conventional points of departure commonly found in tourism research and the incumbent epistemological, ontological and methodological destinations arrived at by researchers. In Sikes' (2006) study, the inspiration for his reflections on issues that have preoccupied him in his intellectual work is a trip to a 'girlie' bar in Bangkok as a tourist. The issues include storying lives, autobiography and/or biography, identities and careers, giving voice, 'Othering', representation, social justice, and making the familiar strange.

HISTORICAL DEVELOPMENT

Autoethnography is a variant of ethnography – a method developed in anthropology for the study of 'other' cultures. Hayano (2001) comments that the turn to autoethnography in anthropology has its genesis in three factors; first, the blurring of otherness by modernisation of even the remotest parts of the world, second, the training of anthropologists from many of the 'other' societies who then conduct fieldwork on their own societies and third, the development of urban anthropology in which students of anthropology are working in their own backyards. The emphasis in the early adoption by anthropologists of autoethnography still lay in extensive fieldwork. Adoption in other fields of study, such as education and health, has introduced other data sources for their research. For example Ellis and Bochner (2000: 77) describe a process 'Systematic sociological introspection and emotional recall' whereby they start research with feelings, thoughts and emotions about a subject and build a narrative through recall, observation and reflection.

DESCRIPTION

The autoethnographic approach tries to answer the question, 'How does my own experience of my own culture offer insights into my culture, situation, event and/or way of life?' (Patton, 2004: 48). The researcher adopts the first-person voice in their writing and may use a number of literary genres: short stories, poetry, fiction, drama, photographic portrayals, personal essays, social science prose. The accounts are written without the pretence of detachment and often combine the deeply personal with the analytical.

POTENTIAL CRITICISM

Autoethnography is controversial in many domains of study. The rejection of objectivity in the stance of the researcher is an obvious start point for social science objection. Reviewers, supervisors and examiners seem to have difficulty with the way Autoethnography deliberately blurs the boundaries found in academic structures and identities. The distinction between, on the one hand, the humanities' emphasis on creativity and, on the other, the rigorous enquiry favoured in the social sciences provides an uncomfortable separation for autoethnographic writing. These objections to Autoethnography have most readily come to the fore in arguments about how to judge its quality. Students may be blocked from pursuing Autoethnography by supervisory panels because it elides notions of validity and reliability in social research. Manuscripts submitted for publication may be subject to very unfavourable reviews if the reviewer applies conventional quality indicators.

In response, practioners of Autoethnography have developed indicators of quality that are appropriate to the approach. For example, Sparkes (2002) reports on a long struggle to have his work published on the sociology of sport literature. He suggests that good Autoethnography is 'heart full'. Elaborating further he suggests that it should include, 'the use of systematic sociological introspection and emotional recall; the inclusion of the researcher's vulnerable selves; ... the celebration of concrete experience and intimate detail; ... the connecting of the practices of social science with the living of life ... ' (Sparkes, 2002: 210).

CROSS REFERENCES

Constructionism, Ethnomethodology, Narrative.

FURTHER READING

Generic

Ellis, C. and Bochner, A.P. (2000) Autoethnography, personal narrative, reflexivity: research as subject, in N.K. Denzin and Y. Lincoln (eds), *Handbook of Qualitative Research*, 2nd edn. Thousand Oaks, CA: Sage. pp. 733–68.

Hayano, D.M. (2001) Auto-ethnography: paradigms, problems, and prospects, in N.K. Denzin and Y.S. Lincoln (eds), *The American Tradition in Qualitative Research*, Vol. III. London: Sage. pp. 122–32.

Patton, M.Q. (2004) Autoethnography, in M. Lewis-Beck, R. Bryman and T.F. Liao (eds), *The SAGE Encyclopaedia of Social Science Research Methods*, Vol. 1. Thousand Oaks, CA: Sage. pp. 46–8.

Sparkes, A.C. (2002) Autoethnography: self-indulgence or something more?, in A.P. Bochner and C. Ellis (eds), *Ethnographically Speaking, Autoethnography, Literature and Aesthetics*. Walnut Creek, CA: Alta Mira. pp. 209–32.

Tourism specific

Botterill, D. (2003) An autoethnographic narrative on tourism research epistemologies, *Loisir et Societe*, 26 (1): 97–110.

Noy, C. (2007a) The language(s) of the tourist experience: an autoethnography of the poetic tourist, in I. Ateljevic, N. Morgan and A. Pritchard (eds), *The Critical Turn*

key concepts in tourism research

in Tourism Studies: Innovative Research Methodologies. Amsterdam: Elsevier Publications. pp. 349–70.

Noy, C. (2007b) The poetics of tourist experience: an autoethnography of a family trip to Eilat, *Journal of Tourism and Cultural Change,* 5 (3): 141–57.

Sikes, P. (2006) Travel broadens the mind or the making of the strange familiar: the story of a visiting academic, *Qualitative Inquiry,* 12 (3): 523–40.

·················· Case Study ··················

> **Definition** The study of a few cases, sometimes one, constructed out of naturally occurring social situations and investigated in considerable depth.

RELEVANCE

As our key concept entry for the Case Study will show you, this is a tried and tested concept in tourism research projects. If you are wanting to study a particular tourism destination then it is an obvious choice, but the Case Study is much more flexible than that. Have a look, below, at the wide range of ways other tourism researchers have used it. An early health warning is needed though to curb enthusiasm for the Case Study. Sometimes the Case Study is used by students as a simple 'catch-all' phrase for any research that is 'selective' but you should avoid this trap and make sure that you make good use of the many guides to selecting and doing Case Study research. It is very important, for example, to choose a case study that is of an appropriate scale for the time and resources available to you and one that is, crucially, accessible. However appealing they may be, exotic case study locations that cannot be practically visited on several occasions during the research project are not a good idea. Similarly, resist the appeal to study your 'home' location, particularly if you are an international student, unless you are absolutely sure you can satisfy the 'access' requirements of your study. Even if you plan to return 'home' during your

case study

19

study period you are likely to want to do many other things rather than pursue your research topic. The Case Study method should never be selected because it a cure for feelings of home sicknesses or as an excuse to visit friends and family during term time! Access to data is absolutely vital but contrary to most students' thinking this does not just depend on conducting interviews. We recommend that you consider a mix of the six sources of evidence that Yin (2003) lists, as a way of demonstrating good Case Study design and as an antidote to the frustration of trying to access busy informants in case study locations, often through a small window of opportunity on a site visit.

APPLICATION

The Case Study dominates the literature of tourism studies as a library search in any tourism database will demonstrate. This is, in part, because the most influential academic disciplines in the emergence of tourism studies were naturally drawn to the Case Study method. The preferred unit of analysis in industrial economics is the 'firm' and first generation tourism scholars drew heavily on their backgrounds in this subset of economics. Subsequently, firm-level analysis has been extended to include many Case Studies of different types of tourism organisation from the smallest micro-businesses to the largest transnational corporation and including the many tiers of government. The Case Study is also the natural territory for another influential discipline in tourism studies – geography. Human geographers were among the first generation of tourism scholars in the UK and in the USA and the emphasis on 'places of tourism' has driven much orthodox thinking in tourism studies, for example in models of tourism destination management and planning including Butler's tourism area life cycle (TALC) model. Given the prevalence of the Case Study in tourism scholarship we should here make a distinction between the Case Study as a research approach and the Case Study as a tool for teaching and learning about tourism. It is the former use of the Case Study that is the focus of our interest.

The sheer volume of research using Case Study approaches makes this a challenging section to write. Rather than point to examples of Case Study research that demonstrate particular characteristics, instead we provide an overview of how Case Study research appears in the tourism literature. So, the inevitable selections we have had to make are only illustrative of general trends in the literature. The dominance of the Case Study approach is clearly demonstrated by edited research monographs in widely divergent topics. For example, in the following monographs, *Tourism, Ethnic Diversity and the City* (Rath, 2007) and *Cultural Tourism, Journeys of Discovery in Volunteer Tourism: International Case Study Perspectives* (Lyons and Wearing, 2007), the Case Study is preferred as a method in over 90 per cent of the chapters.

If we examine how the Case Study approach is used in tourism research it is possible to grasp its full utility. On a descriptive level case studies in specific aspects of tourism are common, see for example nature-based tourism, such as whale watching (Constantine and Bedjer, 2007). There is an extensive use of the Case Study as a research method in studies of tourist consumer behaviour (see for example Lee et al. [2007] on online travel shopping and Laesser [2007] on the use of paper and online promotional materials). This is also true in the tourism management literatures as is demonstrated by studies of wage differentials in the lodging industry (Kline and Hseih, 2007), performance measurement techniques (Phillips and Louvieris, 2005) and how a national tourism promotion agency, VisitScotland, prepared for the Iraq war (Yeoman et al., 2005).

On quite another level, researchers also pose analytical questions and then explore them empirically through a single Case Study. For example Kozak (2007) examines the extent of tourist harassment in Marmaris (Turkey), the adaption strategies of manager/owners in Finland to climate change are reported by Saarinen and Tervo (2005) and Rakic and Chambers (2007) unpick the tensions between national and universal ownership of heritage attractions through an examination of the Acropolis. Single case studies are often reported alongside innovations in method. For example Ahas et al. (2007) use mobile positioning data in studying tourist movement and Garrod (2007) describes how volunteer-employed photography may be used in planning and managing heritage tourism.

Multiple case studies are rarely reported in the literature. Some exceptions to this are Hayden's (2007) study of climate change. Five case studies are presented, each representing a different geographical region, socioeconomic condition and climate. The case study destinations are Australia, Brazil, the European Alps, the Maldives and Southern Europe/the Mediterranean region. Kopinina's (2007) monograph on tourism and migration includes four case studies. As an example of cross case study analysis, then Getz et al. (2004) stands out. Fifteen case studies enable the authors to determine patterns of common characteristics and issues of concern on family businesses in tourism and hospitality.

case study

21

HISTORICAL DEVELOPMENT

Case Study approaches, and there are now several, have their origins in the historical research traditions of medicine and social work. The subsequent prominence of the Case Study in sociology in the 1930s came under intense attack with the rise of quantitative methods in the social sciences. Consequentially, as Hammersley and Gomm (2000) point out, the use of the Case Study has become entangled with the debate on how the social world should be studied and the status given to knowledge of the social world. Some authors have defended the Case Study as a scientific method (for example, Yin, 2003) while others have advanced its claims within the context of a paradigm shift to more naturalistic forms of inquiry (Stake, 1998). The consequent lack of precision on what constitutes a Case Study does not seem to have impeded its popularity, however, and topics as varied as the individual life cycle, organisational and managerial processes, neighbourhood change, international relations and the maturation of industries are abundant in many social science literatures. As we shall see below it is perceived to be particularly dominant in tourism research (Xiao and Smith, 2006).

The imperative to use a Case Study is also divergent. It has been seen as a way of examining the exceptional or deviant and thus challenging orthodox theory or, contrarily, as an archetype that is representative of a wider social morphology. The intention of the researcher may be to investigate a problem in a social context and then do something about it, perhaps to make an intervention in the form of a quasi-experiment. Or a researcher may only be interested in producing a 'thick' description of the case or cases in order to emphasise the unique character of a situation or individual and so on. In this last example it is the pursuit of authenticity of the Case Study that drives the researcher's decision to use the approach. Such approaches may also be used in critical studies to enable previously unheard 'voices' to be represented.

Users of the Case Study also differ in their views about the vexed question of whether Case Study findings are generalisable to a wider population. Much of the argument here is predicated on the (mis)application of criteria devised from statistical inference whereby the representativeness of the case is crucial. Instead, many Case Study researchers argue that generalisability should be based on validity and not representation. Valid generalisation here appeals to logic, analytic induction and to theoretical development (Mitchell, 2000). Further still some researchers contend that Case Study research becomes 'naturalistically generalisable' when results are used by others in their research or practice. Such defence strategies are a staple of standpoint theorists (see Feminism) but they are likely to run into disputes over any claim to 'authenticity' that is fuelled by the postmodernist attack on the real and upon any attempt at a meta-narrative interpretation of the social world.

DESCRIPTION

The starting point for all researchers using a Case Study is to decide on the unit of analysis. This involves decisions on the boundaries of the Case Study under examination. These may be spatial (a neighbourhood, town, or region), temporal (a particular era or period) or structural (a particular human condition, a group, an institution, a piece of legislation, organisation or department). A Case Study approach can take on different designs depending upon the thrust of the research question. One unit of analysis results in a single Case Study design, two interconnecting units of analysis suggest a comparative Case Study design and a larger constituency of units provides a multiple Case Study design. Case Study researchers have a wide range of data sources to choose from. Yin (2003) identifies six: documentation, archival records, interviews, direct observation, participant observation and physical artefacts.

POTENTIAL CRITICISM

The criticisms of the Case Study approach concern the claims that may be made for the generalisation of research findings. The argument here is that any number of Case Studies cannot enable analysis that results in consistent and replicable results. There are two responses to these criticisms. The first is to argue for a different kind of generalisation from Case Study research. The arguments of Stake (1998) and Guba and Lincoln (1989) are that it is up to the reader of the reported Case Study to assess the generalisability of the findings by reference to their own investigations or experiences. This is assisted by a commitment to reporting 'thick description' to facilitate the comparability of the studied cases. While accepting this as helpful, Gomm et al. (2000) still regard these responses as giving too much weight to the critics of Case Study research and instead Gomm and his colleagues produce a valiant attempt to justify empirical generalisations from (1) studied to unstudied cases and (2) within Case Study generalisation. They mount this on the basis of calling for the use of additional data that provides indications of the heterogeneity of the population as a context in which empirical generalisations may be drawn. They also insist on greater care with case study selection or sampling and suggest systematic sampling and cumulative case study building as defensible strategies. Xiao and Smith (2006) conclude their review of the Case Study in tourism research by reviewing this 'generalisation' debate within the context of a Content Analysis study of 78 articles appearing in four tourism journals over a five-year period.

CROSS REFERENCES

Document Analysis, Evaluation Research, Grounded Theory.

FURTHER READING

Generic

Guba, E. and Lincoln, Y.S. (1989) *Fourth Generation Evaluation*. Newbury Park, CA: Sage.

Hammersley, M. and Gomm, R. (2000) Introduction, in R. Gomm, M. Hammersley and P. Foster (eds), *Case Study Method*. Thousand Oaks, CA: Sage. pp. 1–16.

Mitchell, J.C. (2000) Case and situation analysis, in R. Gomm, M. Hammersley and P. Foster (eds), *Case Study Method*. Thousand Oaks, CA: Sage. pp. 165–86.

Stake, R.E. (1998) Case studies, in N.K Denzin and Y.S. Lincoln (eds), *Strategies of Qualitative Inquiry*. Thousand Oaks, CA: Sage. pp. 86–109.

Yin, R.K. (2003) *Case Study Research: Design and Methods*. 3rd edn. London: Thousand Oaks, CA: Sage.

Tourism specific

Ahas, R., Aasa, A., Mark, Ü., Pae, T. and Kull, A. (2007) Seasonal tourism spaces in Estonia: case study with mobile positioning data, *Tourism Management*, 28 (3): 898–910.

Constantine, R. and Bedjer, L. (2007) Managing the whale- and dolphin-watching industry, in J. Higham and M. Lück (eds), *Marine Wildlife and Tourism Management; Insights from the Natural and Social Sciences*. Oxford: CABI. pp. 321–33.

Daher, R.F. (ed) (2006) *Tourism in the Middle East: Continuity, Change and Transformation*. Clevedon: Channel View Publications.

Garrod, B. (2007) A snapshot into the past: the utility of volunteer-employed photography in planning and managing heritage tourism, *Journal of Heritage Tourism*, 2 (1): 14–35.

Getz, D., Carlsen, J. and Morrison, A. (2004) Cross-case analysis, in D. Getz, J. Carlsen and A. Morrison (eds), *The Family Business in Tourism and Hospitality*. Oxford: CABI. pp. 161–71.

Hayden, L. (2007) Tourism and climate change, *Travel & Tourism Analyst*, 1: 1–37.

Kline, S. and Hseih, Y.C. (2007) Wage differentials in the lodging industry: a case study, *Journal of Human Resources in Hospitality & Tourism*, 6: 69–84.

Kozak, M. (2007) Tourist harassment: a marketing perspective, *Annals of Tourism Research*, 34 (2): 384–99.

Laesser, C. (2007) There is a market for destination brochures – but is there a future? *Tourism Review*, 62 (3/4): 27–31.

Lee, H.Y., Qu, H.L. and Kim, Y.S. (2007) A study of the impact of personal innovativeness on online travel shopping behavior – a case study of Korean travellers, *Tourism Management*, 28 (3): 886–97.

Lyons, K.D. and Wearing, S. (eds) (2007) *Cultural Tourism, Journeys of Discovery in Volunteer Tourism: International Case Study Perspectives*. Oxford: CABI.

Kopinina, H. (2007) *Tourism and Migration: Formation of New Social Classes*. New York: Cognizant Comunication Corp.

Phillips P. and Louvieris, P. (2005) Performance measurement systems in tourism, hospitality, and leisure small and medium-sized enterprises: a balanced scorecard perspective, *Journal of Travel Research*, 44 (2): 201–11.

Rakic, T. and Chambers, D. (2007) World heritage: exploring the tension between the national and the 'universal', *Journal of Heritage Tourism*, 2 (3): 145–55.

Rath, J. (2007) *Tourism, Ethnic Diversity and the City*. London: Routledge.

Saarinen, J. and Tervo, K. (2005) Perceptions and adaption strategies of the tourism industry to climate change: the case of Finnish nature-based tourism entrepreneurs, *International Journal of Innovation & Sustainable Development*, 1 (3): 214–28.

Xiao, H. and Smith, S.L.J. (2006) Case studies in tourism research: a state-of-the-art analysis, *Tourism Management*, 27: 738–49.

Yeoman, I., Galt, M. and McMahon-Beattie, U. (2005) A case study of how VisitScotland prepared for war, *Journal of Travel Research*, 44 (1): 6–20.

Constructionism

Definition A philosophical position whereby the meaning of the social world is not discovered but is constructed by history, society, ideas and language.

RELEVANCE

We can easily understand the appeal that Constructionism has for tourism students, particularly for those who are required to engage with the philosophy of social science by their supervisors. It offers both a firm basis from which to undertake your research project and an invitation to escape the normalised strictures of 'doing' social scientific research. It invites creativity and challenges the notion of what constitutes 'data'. For many students of tourism, the idea of letting their research speak through the constructions of respondents is very appealing and the use of something other than words or numbers to represent the respondent 'voice', or the topic under investigation, has a liberating, feel-good, democratising factor. In this respect, the exploitation of visual representations of data, so central to the practice and process of tourism, seems a 'natural' choice. Two initial sentiments of caution, first, Constructionism implies a commitment to researcher reflexivity. You should be prepared to open up yourself as a researcher in your writing with just as much candour as you expect from your respondents, or if you prefer the term, your co-researchers. Second, the liberation from the strictures of normative scientific process means that there are many less tried and tested ways of doing research, less rules and conventions to guide you, and in our experience some student researchers find this uncomfortable to say the least. Consequentially, you will need to develop a confident and rigorous defence of your own research strategy and be prepared to defend your work if it is attacked. This can only be achieved by extensive reading around the philosophies of the social sciences, there is no short cut here. Finally, you should read the potential criticisms section below to counterbalance the appeal and popularity of Constructionism with what are its quite severe limitations.

APPLICATION

The turn to Constructionism in tourism research is reported both directly as a meta-theoretical proposition and indirectly through the incorporation of a range of data sources and methods. Hollinshead (2006) and Tribe (2006) both concentrate on the implications of a turn to social constructionism in their meta-theoretical critiques of tourism knowledge. The incumbent methodological preoccupations with 'reflexivity', 'voice', 'text', 'participant involvement' and 'audience' are discussed in a generic sense by Crouch (2005), Hollingshead and Jamal (2007) and by Westwood et al. (2006). Also in this vein of scholarship is Pritchard and Morgan's (2006) invitation to re-explore the term 'hotel' as a social construct.

However, the 'turn' to Constructionism in tourism research is most strongly evidenced in studies that are based on a new range of data sources. Visual material is particularly well represented in studies that explore the social construction of tourism (see also Visual Methods). For example, Shandley et al. (2006) and Law et al. (2007) study the interplay between film and tourism development, Brett (1994) uses art and photography to examine the influence of tourism on Irish culture, Pritchard and Morgan (2005a) compare postcards and art in denigrating the Welsh as a marginal ethnic minority, Dunn (2005) explores the social meaning of Venice through television programmes, and several authors mine the print media for inspiration (see, for example, Pritchard and Morgan, 2005b). Tribe's (2008) article on 'the art of tourism' exemplifies the possibilities of Constructionism for both its proponents and its detractors. Although visual material dominates constructionist studies, tourism scholars are also exploring literature, text and music. Scholars at the Centre for Cultural Change and Tourism have considered the interplay between tourism and literature (Robinson and Andersen, 2002; Robinson, 2005), music (Wheeller, 2005) and the material culture of festivals (Picard, 2006).

Constructionism has also invited a greater attention to the accounts of tourists, employees, residents and individuals from many other social groupings involved with tourism. The plethora of voices speaking about tourism that are recorded in the tourism literature is largely due to the constructionist turn. Typical examples include Li et al. (2010) on international tourists' experiences, Weaver (2009) on graduates' views of the quality of jobs in tourism, Keiti et al. (2008) on the aspirations of the Kenyan poor for tourism development, and Yates' (2007) study of disabled tourists.

HISTORICAL DEVELOPMENT

Constructionism's rise to prominence in the social sciences in the later part of the 20th century derives from two directions. First, and somewhat surprisingly perhaps, the study of sub-atomic physics and, second, the mounting resistance to the adoption of naturalism in the social sciences. Developments in the study of sub-atomic physics in the 1950s and 1960s opened a fissure in the naturalist's own arguments about the realness of the physical world. The presumption that the natural world contains regularities, patterns and recurrences, and that inductive methods can expose them, came under intense scrutiny as natural scientists deepened the level of inquiry. Experiments at the sub-atomic level revealed a new level of complexity and paradox and natural scientists have conceded that at least at some levels of analysis, reality in the natural world may not be characterised by regularity and pattern. Among the new conditions confronting science was the question of the neutrality of researcher intervention in measurement, as captured by Heisenberg's uncertainty principle (see, for example, Capra, 1982). These perplexing turns in natural science have found expression in a new raft of theorising characterised by chaos and complexity theory.

As these revelations began to filter out to the wider academic community, social scientists who had emulated the methods of the natural sciences realised that the previously solid ground of naturalism was subject to an internal critique of its fundamental premises. It is not surprising then that those social scientists who had always been uncomfortable with the emulation of natural science should have renewed their arguments for a separation between the natural and social sciences with more vigour.

Pre-dating this 20th century challenge to naturalist principles, the adoption of the methods of natural science in social science had proved controversial. The doubts about the natural world at sub-atomic levels opened a crack for intensifying the argument that the social world presents itself as fundamentally different from the natural world in a number of ways. If there are patterns in the social world then they are more fleeting and contextualised. The possibility that they are subjectively and not objectively observed raised doubts about the 'realness' of social life. Furthermore the reflexive, creative and intentional characteristic of the social world provides a set of conditions that demand very different epistemological and methodological response.

The philosophical anchor of Constructionism is found in Kant's philosophy of knowledge. Kant refused to accept the 'tabula rasa' condition of the mind, presumed in naturalism. He accepted sense perception as a way to knowledge of the world but rejected the idea that the mind simply received these stimuli. Instead he argued that it was the mind that organised and categorised the sense data into patterns and regularities. Furthermore, he asserted that there are a common set of categories of mind that correspond to what we understand it means to be human. Ideas about the world are therefore not anchored in the world but are anchored in the mind. Induced patterns and regularities do not reside in the real world but reside in the mind. So it follows that under Constructionism claims about the properties of the social world are limited by our perceptions of the world – how it appears to us – a world of phenomena. Kant's philosophy of knowledge therefore set up a new territory for exploring how those perceptions have been formulated. Indeed it provided the basis for a whole new raft of ideas in the humanities and subsequently in the social sciences and ultimately fuelled a rift between the natural and social sciences. Recognising the constructed nature of social knowledge is the starting point for many accounts that seek to rid social inquiry of rigid certainties. Central to this project is the question of 'What have been the historical, social, ideological and linguistic influences upon perceptions of the social world?' (Moses and Knutsen, 2007).

DESCRIPTION

Constructionism required a very different and diffuse methodology to that pursued in the natural sciences. If history, society, ideas and language construct the meanings that are ascribed to the objects of investigation, then there are clearly limits to what the social sciences might have to say about patterns and regularities in the external 'real' social world. Indeed constructionist scholarship is reduced to demonstrating what regularities exist in social scientific 'accounts' of the real world. In pursuing Constructionism it became necessary, therefore, to relax the rules of scientific enquiry but in accepting a presupposition – that we cannot observe anything without a frame of reference – social scientists needed to devise reflexive methodologies, those in which interpretations of the social world are always understood within one's own frame of reference.

This does not necessarily lead to an abandonment of objectivity in inquiry, instead it requires that the pursuit of objectivity becomes an examination of the influences over our sensory perceptions. It is here that the imperative for reflexivity in research is formulated because the examination of influences over the research process foregrounds the influences over the researcher's sensory perceptions. This radical shift in social research, inspired by Constructionism, has produced great diversity in the methods and the reporting of social research. No longer constrained by the neutrality of naturalistic methods, the researcher is encouraged to 'insert' themselves whole heartedly into the research and to even report in the previously demonised 'I' form, or first person writing style. Thus the relationship between social scientists' ideas about reality and reality itself is additionally confounded by the web of meanings mediated through the language of everyday life.

Constructionism challenged the privileging within science of reason, head, mechanics, the impersonal and order. Instead, its supporters argued that if social science was to capture the fleeting and subjective it needed to embrace other aspects of human experience: the heart, the spiritual, the deeply personal and the dynamic chaos of the social condition. These challenges to scientific epistemology brought the social sciences closer to the methods of the humanities and fuelled post-structuralist analysis that included representations of social life, as in for example, the novel, play or poetry, as legitimate ways to capture insight into the social condition (see Autoethnography).

Constructionist work has spurned a range of new social research methods that defy a simple listing. Gergen (2004) usefully categorises them by their contribution to constructionist social science. He reminds us that they emphasise:

- value reflections (who is advantaged, or exploited, by the method?);
- subject voice (is the voice of the subject heard?);
- collaborative participation (do the subjects collaborate in knowledge production?);
- multiple standpoints (are multiple standpoints and values represented?)
- representational creativity (not limited to formal writing, can include visual and aural).

The image of the researcher that is conjured up by reading constructivist accounts is far removed from the white-coated, detached and unemotional researcher. Instead it is replaced by a metaphor of the 'researcher as bricoleur' (Crotty, 1998: 51), as someone with a fascination with objects but who is not constrained or straightjacketed by the conventional meanings we have been taught to associate with the object. The constructionist researcher, therefore, operates within a radical spirit of openness that leads to creative reinterpretations of the objects of our social world.

POTENTIAL CRITICISM

The fissure in the certainties of naturalism and the scientific method has not rebuffed the critics of Constructionism. The pluralism of method, of data and of research design has provided ammunition for critics who ask the question, 'How can we judge what is and what is not a "good" research design?' Their arguments contend that if there is no 'standard' or authority on methods, then how will contributions to scientific knowledge be evaluated?

This question is in part answered by constructionists to varying degrees by stressing a demarcation between methods. Some 'weak' constructionists argue for a demarcation based on the 'appropriateness' of method, although the difficulty of defining appropriateness remains. The 'strong' constructionists, including postmodernists, simply dismiss the question and reject any kind of demarcation of science from any other form of knowledge. In one of the fiercest attacks on the supposed superiority of the scientific method, Feyerbend (1975) argues that science has no special features that render it intrinsically superior to other kinds of knowledge such as ancient myths or voodoo. Instead he suggests that aesthetic criteria, personal whims and social factors have had a decisive role in the history of science. From his standpoint, alternative epistemologies provide a choice between scientific knowledge and other forms of knowledge and it follows that democratic control of science should necessarily follow. Science should not place a stranglehold on knowledge and individuals should be emancipated to chose between the various claims to truth.

CROSS REFERENCES

Autoethnography, Content Analysis, Document Analysis, Hermeneutics, Narrative, Post-colonialism, Postmodernism, Repertory Grid, Visual Methods.

FURTHER READING

Generic

Capra, F. (1982) *The Turning Point: Science, Society and the Rising Culture.* New York: Simon and Schuster.

Crotty, M. (1998) *The Foundations of Social Research: Meanings and Perspectives in the Research Process.* London: Sage.

Feyerbend, P. (1975) *Against Method.* London: Verso.

Gergen, K.J. (2004) Constructionism, social, in M. Lewis-Beck, R. Bryman and T.F. Liao (eds), *The SAGE Encyclopaedia of Social Science Research Methods*, Vol. 1. Thousand Oaks, CA: Sage. pp. 183–5.

Moses, J.W. and Knutsen, T.L. (2007) *Ways of Knowing: Competing Methodologies in Social and Political Research*. Basingstoke: Palgrave Macmillan.

Tourism specific

Brett. D. (1994) The representation of culture, in U. Kockel (ed.), *Culture, Tourism and Development: The Case of Ireland*. Liverpool: Liverpool University Press. pp. 117–28.

Crouch, D. (2005) Tourism research practices and tourist geographies, in B.W. Ritchie, P. Burns and C. Palmer (eds), *Tourism Research Methods: Integrating Theory with Practice*. Oxford: CABI. pp. 73–84.

Dunn, D. (2005) Venice observed: the traveller, the tourist, the post-tourist and British television, in A. Jaworski and A. Pritchard (eds), *Discourse, Communication and Tourism*. Clevedon: Channel View. pp. 98–120.

Hollinshead, K. (2006) The shift to constructivism in social inquiry: some pointers for tourism studies, *Tourism Recreation Research*, 31 (2): 43–58.

Hollinshead K. and Jamal T.B. (2007) Tourism and the third ear: further prospects for qualitative inquiry, *Tourism Analysis*, 12 (1/2): 85–129.

Kieti, D.M., Jones, E. and Wishitemi, B. (2008) Alternative models of community tourism: balancing economic development and the aspirations of the poor, *Tourism Review International*, 12 (3/4): 275–90.

Law, L., Bunnell, T. and Ong, C.E. (2007) *The Beach*, the gaze and film tourism, *Tourist Studies*, 7 (2): 141–64.

Li, M.Z., Duncan, T., Kline, C. and Schneider, P. (2010) The voyage of the self: experiencing the subjective zone of international travel, *Annals of Leisure Research*, 13 (1/2): 191–217.

Picard, D. (2006) Gardening the past and being in the world: a popular celebration of the abolition of slavery in *La Réunion*, in D. Picard and M. Robinson (eds), *Festivals, Tourism and Social Change: Remaking Worlds*. Clevedon: Channel View. pp. 46–70.

Pritchard, A. and Morgan, N. (2005a) Representations of 'ethnographic knowledge': early comic postcards of Wales, in A. Jaworski and A. Pritchard (eds), *Discourse, Communication and Tourism*, Clevedon: Channel View. pp. 53–75.

Pritchard, A. and Morgan, N. (2005b) On location: re(viewing) bodies of fashion and places of desire, *Tourist Studies*, 5 (3): 283–302.

Pritchard, A. and Morgan, N. (2006) Hotel Babylon? Exploring hotels as liminal sites of transition and transgression, *Tourism Management*, 27 (5): 762–72.

Robinson, M. (2005) The trans-textured tourist: literature as knowledge in the making of tourists, *Tourism Recreation Research*, 30 (1): 73–81.

Robinson, M. and Andersen, H.C. (eds) (2002) *Literature and Tourism: Reading and Writing Tourism Texts*. London: Thompson Learning.

Shandley, R., Jamal, T. and Tanase, A. (2006) Location shooting and the filmic destination: Transylvanian myths and the post-colonial tourism enterprise, *Journal of Tourism and Cultural Change*, 4 (3): 137–58.

Tribe, J. (2006) The truth about tourism, *Annals of Tourism Research*, 33 (2): 360–81.

Tribe, J. (2008) The art of tourism, *Annals of Tourism Research*, 35 (4): 924–44.

Weaver, A. (2009) Perceptions of job quality in the tourism industry: the views of recent graduates of a university's tourism management programme, *International Journal of Contemporary Hospitality Management*, 21 (5): 579–93.

Westwood, S., Morgan, N. and Pritchard, A. (2006) Situation, participation and reflexivity in tourism research: furthering interpretive approaches to tourism enquiry, *Tourism Recreation Research*, 31 (2): 33–4.

Wheeller, B. (2005) The king is dead. Long live the product: Elvis, authenticity, sustainability and the product life cycle, in R.W. Butler (ed.), *The Tourism Area Life Cycle, Vol. 1: Applications and Modifications*. Clevedon: Channel View. pp. 339–47.

Yates, K. (2007) Understanding the experiences of mobility-disabled tourists, *International Journal of Tourism Policy*, 1 (2): 153–66.

Content Analysis

Definition Content Analysis is a research technique for making replicable and valid inferences from text or image.

RELEVANCE

This is a great place to start if you are looking for a project that makes use of existing data, particularly if it is in word or image format. There is a tremendous amount of information about tourism now readily available in digitised format and while it is our experience that students of tourism are generally quite socially adept and are keen to interact with others to build their empirical evidence, if you would prefer not to encounter other people in collecting data then Content Analysis is an excellent way to go. It requires a different skill-set and more than likely will tax your willingness to stare at a screen and 'study' as opposed to some other diversionary, more appealing, 'app'. Remember, too, that the volume of material that is out there results in many sampling challenges to confront and, as you have not collected the data yourself, then questions about its reliability and validity might be difficult to answer satisfactorily.

content analysis

33

APPLICATION

The emergence in tourism studies of the digital and the visual are encouraging the adoption of Content Analysis. This is exemplified in the increasing number of published studies that use websites as source material. The emphasis may be on web-design (see Roney and Özturan [2006] on travel agency website design) or on inference between media representation and published strategic or social goals. For example, Antum et al. conducted a study of ethnic diversity in the workplace by examining the websites of 100 restaurant corporations from which they conclude 'most of the firms' web sites provided little or no concrete evidence of the firms' active commitment to diversity. Furthermore, the study revealed "disconnects" between the intended message of being an equal opportunity employer and the actual message' (2007: 85).

The plethora of visual materials associated with tourism has been mined extensively using Content Analysis. Page et al. (2006) examine photographic images of adventure tourism brochures, Okumas et al. (2007) use images from both print and web to investigate images of food in tourism marketing and Eagles and Wind (1994) combine image and text analysis of ecotour company offerings.

Content Analysis has also been employed to sharpen the conceptual development of tourism studies, for example two studies investigate the definition of ecotourism (Donohoe and Needham, 2006; Garrod, 2003), and Xiao and Smith (2006) use Content Analysis to rebuff criticism of an over dependency on Case Study in tourism research. The adoption of Content Analysis in tourism studies displays a marked incremental sophistication in technique from, for example, Dilley's (1986) then ground-breaking but now naive study of brochure image to the analysis of promotional materials of Macau using text mining/expert judgement and correspondence analysis conducted by Choi et al. (2007). A classic example of Content Analysis is provided by Nickerson (1995) who conducted:

> A newspaper content analysis of tourism and gambling in Deadwood, South Dakota (USA) [that] provides information on the issues portrayed to the general public about gaming. In five years, 712 articles written in three local newspapers portrayed five general categories of information: economics, regulatory concerns, initial questions on gaming, logistics and planning needed, and negative attitudes toward gaming. (Nickerson, 1995: 53)

HISTORICAL DEVELOPMENT

The revolution in communication inspired by the technology of the printing press in the 16th century was quickly followed by the practice of Content Analysis and the censorship of religious texts. However, the term Content Analysis first entered the English language in 1941 (Krippendorf, 2004). Its emergence as a specific technique in the era of the printed word concentrated on the measurement of column inches and the quantification of word counts. The movement from 'counting regimes' to 'inference' followed the application of Content Analysis in the interrogation of propaganda as a method for anticipating, or inferring, enemy strategy in the Second World War.

The popularisation of visual communication in the second half of the 20th century through the technologies and industrial structures surrounding film and television, extended the use of the technique to visual material. Topics such as the analysis of stereotypes and style, symbols and values moved Content Analysis further away from its simple counting methods and aligned the method with more general questions in the social sciences of how society operates and how it understands itself through its texts. Thus, social scientists and humanities scholars from different disciplines – anthropology, sociology, and history – led a general shift away from content measurement to an exploration of social meanings.

Computerised analysis of text moved quickly from its obvious strength for counting frequency to becoming a part of interactive hermeneutical text analysis. The methods of discourse analysis, rhetoric, and conversational analysis adapted to the potential of relational computer software such as NVivo and Nud*ist as a way of exploring the meanings of text. It is common nowadays to find Content Analysis in studies that draw upon critical theory and literary theory, as it has evolved into a repertoire of methods of research that promise to yield inferences from verbal, pictorial, symbolic and communication data.

DESCRIPTION

In all applications of Content Analysis the researcher operates a coding scheme (Neuendorf, 2002). Here the researcher identifies the frequency of particular words, phrases or images and places them in a number of categories. Simple counts of frequency are then easily calculated. It is often the case that the volume of source material exceeds the capacity of the researcher and a sampling technique is required. Analysis of the categories produces the most common results of Content Analysis through the identification of themes. However, the complexity of 'meaning' portrayed in text and image requires a more subtle phase of analysis. Researchers using Content Analysis are confronted with multiple layers of meaning that emerge from an examination of the backgrounding and foregrounding of the information, the silences and emphases in the material and the selection of descriptions of phenomena. Semantic or referential content analysis attempts to capture the nuances inherent in the source material.

POTENTIAL CRITICISM

A major criticism of Content Analysis refers to the reliability of the coding process. The question posed is, 'would different coders come up with different results?'. Additionally, some observers of Content Analysis are unimpressed by the volumes of data driven by the method and claim that the extension of Content Analysis from simple frequency counts to inferences about relationships between themes are insufficiently rigorous. They ask whether the 'analysis' simply reflects the researcher's preoccupations and they challenge the validity of findings. Roberts (2001) addresses this issue by reference to historical debates on Content Analysis method that draws a distinction between representational and instrumental interpretation. In the former the categories are claimed to have been derived from the source and in the latter they are derived from the researcher's theoretical frame.

CROSS REFERENCES

Constructionism, Document Analysis, Ethnomethodology, Hermeneutics, Narrative.

FURTHER READING

Generic

Krippendorff, K. (2004) *Content Analysis: An Introduction to its Methodology*, 2nd edn. Thousand Oaks, CA: Sage.
Neuendorf, K.A. (2002) *The Content Analysis Guidebook*. Thousand Oaks, CA: Sage.
Roberts, C.W. (2001) Content analysis, in N.J. Smelser and Paul B. Baltes (eds), *International Encyclopedia of the Social and Behavioural Sciences*, Vol. 4. Oxford: Elsevier. pp. 2697–702.

Tourism specific

Antun, J.M., Strick, S. and Thomas, L. (2007) Exploring culture and diversity for Hispanics in restaurant online recruitment efforts, *Journal of Human Resources in Hospitality & Tourism*, 6 (1): 85–107.
Choi, S.J., Lehto, X.Y. and Morrison, A.M. (2007) Destination image representation on the web: content analysis of Macau travel related websites, *Tourism Management*, 28 (1): 118–29.

Dilley, R.S. (1986) Tourist brochures and tourist images, *Canadian Geography*, 30 (1): 59–65.

Donohoe, H.M. and Needham, R.D. (2006) Ecotourism: the evolving contemporary definition, *Journal of Ecotourism*, 5 (2): 190–210.

Eagles, P.F.J. and Wind, E. (1994) Canadian ecotours in 1992: a content analysis of advertising, *Journal of Applied Recreation Research*, 19 (1): 67–87.

Garrod, B. (2003) Defining marine ecotourism: a Delphi study, in B. Garrod and J.C. Wilson (eds), *Marine Ecotourism: Issues and Experiences*. Clevedon: Channel View. pp. 17–36.

Okumus, B., Okumus, F. and McKercher, B. (2007) Incorporating local and international cuisines in the marketing of tourism destinations: the cases of Hong Kong and Turkey, *Tourism Management*, 28 (1): 253–261.

Nickerson, N.P. (1995) Tourism and gambling content analysis, *Annals of Tourism Research*, 22 (1): 53–66.

Page, S.J., Steele, W. and Connell, J. (2006) Analysing the promotion of adventure tourism: a case of Scotland, *Journal of Sport Tourism*, 11 (1): 51–76.

Roney, S.A. and Özturan, M. (2006) A content analysis of the web sites of Turkish travel agencies, *Anatolia*, 17 (1): 43–54.

Xiao, H. and Smith, S.L.J. (2006) The maturation of tourism research: evidence from a content analysis, *Tourism Analysis*, 10: 335–48.

Critical Realism

> **Definition** Critical Realism is a way of understanding the natural and human sciences that is committed to the view that the objects of scientific knowledge both exist and act independently of our beliefs about them but, at the same time, rejects simple 'one to one' links between beliefs and reality (Benton, 2004).

RELEVANCE

If you are drawn to Critical Realism, then the challenge you face will be to directly confront the language of the philosophies of the social sciences as a part of your research project. The priority such activity will have in terms of time allocation and resolve to master quite complex material will probably depend on the academic level at which you are studying tourism. In our opinion, this key concept is crucial to the future of tourism knowledge and if you have ambitions towards making an academic contribution from your research project, perhaps in the form of a research article, then getting to grips with Critical Realism and the other cross-referenced key concepts is an investment that will pay dividends in the long run.

APPLICATION

There are very few explicit references to Critical Realism in the tourism studies literature although there is a burgeoning of tourism research that is unselfconsciously both critical and realist. In part, this is because although diversity of method and methodology has been evidenced in tourism research (see Constructionism) engagement with the philosophy of social science has for the most part been implicit, and by default, rather than explicit, and by intention. Where authors have engaged with the philosophy of social science then their interpretations of Realism and in particular of Critical Realism have proved to be somewhat misleading. For example, Hollinshead (2004) identifies four competing schools of thought within contemporary tourist studies (see also Jamal and Everett, 2004), following the lead of Guba (1990) on pre-paradigms in social science, namely:

- *positivism*, which borrows from the natural sciences in employing 'the closed internal logic of mathematics' (Botterill, 2003: 100) to obtain knowledge of the social world via sense experience, that is derived from discrete, atomistic, observed events (i.e. positive facts, not normative values); this knowledge is of patterns in those events that take the form of regularities or constant conjunctions (i.e. if x occurs then y will also occur, notwithstanding exceptions to the rule in question brought about by extraneous factors), and should have the potential to address and solve real-life problems;
- *constructivism*, a reaction to the above that redistributes the power to explain and be explained in favour of the observed over the observer, leading to multiple realities that are inseparable from those who apprehend them and which can only be understood through interpretation (hermeneutics), not observation (i.e. qualitative instead of quantitative methods);
- *critical theory*, its ideologically oriented standpoints (e.g. Marxism, feminism) allowing for research that contains the potential to emancipate the subject from exploitation and oppression; and

- *post-positivism* (also known as *realism*), in which reality is taken to exist but never fully apprehended, thus knowledge of it is both fallible and critical.

The second, third and fourth schools of thought each represent a distinctive break with the first and, in most disciplines/subject areas, approximate to the competing paradigms that have contested the intellectual space wrested from it in the wake of the 'cultural turn' in the social sciences. Of course, the balance of power varies from discipline to discipline and subject area to subject area. In tourism studies the first remains dominant but under increasing attack, the second is emergent and becoming the orthodoxy, and the third is growing. The fourth, here labelled 'post-positivism', should be more correctly aligned with positivism and is dominant in tourism studies but, as we report in the sections on Critical Realism and Realism in this book, studies following the tenets of the misplaced 'Realism' are rare. These trends are perpetuated, to a degree, by the inclination of colleagues in the subject area who have been seduced by the popularity of postmodern or anti-Enlightenment conceptions, to position the debate as between quantitative and qualitative approaches (Phillimore and Goodson, 2004) or, alternatively, 'naturalistic' (realist) and 'progressivist' (antirealist) frames of reference (after Holliday, 2002; cited in Hollinshead, 2004).

In the analyses of Hollinshead (2004) and Jamal and Everett (2004), post-positivism/realism is subsumed under quantitative as a less 'radical' and, by implication, inadequate reaction to the excesses of the Enlightenment Project, given that it shares with positivism a belief in the unity of the natural and social sciences and a reality that is separate from our conceptions of it. What Hollinshead and others have not acknowledged is that Realism rejects outright the positivist methodology of 'observation + correlation = explanation + prediction'. Consequently, and in our view incorrectly, these authors come to assume that Constructivism and Critical Theory are the only alternatives to positivism. This is further reinforced by Hollinshead who, following Guba (1990), conflates positivism with post-positivism and, thus, closes down on any realist analysis as 'constrained by the technical efficacy and the imperatives of instrumental action within organisations' (Hollinshead, 2004: 77).

We acknowledge that the paradigm debate was a valuable development in the social sciences, but that to simplify is to risk misrepresentation, especially as Kuhn developed the notion of paradigms 'at a time when there was greater rigidity and structure in academic subject areas' (Cooper, 2003: 2). Realist social science in its post-positivist phase, to use Hollinshead's terminology, is very far removed from positivism (Sayer, 2004a), thus it is mistaken to conflate realism with post-positivism. Indeed, in reinstating the distinction between causal mechanisms, or what causes something to happen, and empirical regularities, or the number of times something happens, realism is not simply post-positivist, it is *anti*-positivist (Stockmann, 1983). Despite the welcome intentions of some tourism authors to engage with the philosophies of the social sciences the persistent use of post-positivist to categorise Critical Realism is unfortunate to say the least (see, for example, Pernecky and Jamal, 2010). Furthermore, while the pre-paradigmatic debates capture the recent past, current debates in the philosophy of social science indicate a much more dynamic dispute between two main philosophical positions, Constructionism and Critical Realism (Delanty, 1997). One quite sharp distinction between these positions is that the former champions qualitative approaches, while the latter is open-ended on matters of methodology and method (Carter and New, 2004).

One of the few explicit demonstrations of critical realist tourism research is provided by Gale and Botterill in which they propose:

> a (critical) realist agenda for tourist studies, centred around the question 'What makes tourism possible?' In asserting realism as the philosophy of social science most likely to advance tourism theory, it offers a critique of prevailing epistemologies, notably positivism and constructivism (and critical theory), with a view to provoking engagement by the tourism research community with ontological and epistemological argument. (2005: 151)

HISTORICAL DEVELOPMENT

Critical Realism 'offers an alternative both to the spurious scientificity of positivism and to idealist and relativist reactions to postmodernity' (Sayer, 2004b: 6). As a complete philosophy of, and for, the social sciences, it is gaining ground in a number of influencing disciplines in the study of tourism, for example, economics, sociology, and organisation and management studies. Originating from the writings of Bhaskar (1978, 1979) on 'transcendental realism' (his general philosophy of science) and 'critical naturalism' (his specific philosophy of the human sciences), critical realism challenges the dominant approaches of positivism and hermeneutics by defending the power of both natural *and* social science to *explain*, as well as *observe* and *interpret*. Critical Realism relies on three underlying philosophical tenets: a differentiated and stratified ontology; epistemic relativism; and judgemental rationality.

DESCRIPTION

To be realist is to hold to the view that there is a mind-independent external reality and that it can be known. Exploring and understanding the nature of that reality becomes the primary purpose of realist thinkers. Critical realists, therefore, foreground ontology over epistemology, and much of the social scientific critical realist project is founded upon an examination of 'What makes society possible?'. Consequentially, the central question for Gale and Botterill (2005) of their realist project asks 'What makes tourism possible?'. Furthermore, critical realism proposes a differentiated ontology of social reality divided into the 'transitive domain' (our theories, concepts and discourse of research) and the 'intransitive domain' (the largely enduring structures and properties of objects that enable and constrain human agency).

The realist claim to a mind-independent world does not presuppose some simplistic privileged access to social reality but, rather, a much more complex interaction in which theoretical categories inform, and are informed by, empirical materials (Gregory, 1982). This, in turn, produces fallibilist, practically adequate claims to truth based on judgemental rationality. We need, also, to refer here to another important position in the ontology of critical realism that not only distinguishes between the world and our experience of it, but also proposes a stratified ontology structured into: (1) the empirical; (2) the actual; and (3) the generative mechanisms. Here, Bhaskar (1978: 13) was referring to the notion that knowledge of the social world is stratified into: (1) surface or experiential knowledge; (2) events that happen whether we experience them or not; and (3) a further depth strata that produces the events in the world that is comprised of what might, metaphorically, be called *mechanisms*. This deep strata should not be simply conflated with social reality as it has a distinct ontological character, and it is what distinguishes critical realism from previous manifestations of realism (see, for example, Fleetwood and Ackroyd, 2004). Crucially, these mechanisms:

- are hidden from the gaze of the casual observer, yet are no less real than that which can be sensed;
- are *circumstantial* rather than deterministic or, to be specific, they possess causal powers that may or may not be activated, depending on contingently related conditions (Sayer, 2001); and
- comprise a reality that is *not* a construct of a reflexive or self-referential science, despite the fact that it can only be known in terms of the discourses available to us (which is why our theories concerning that reality are, of necessity, fallible and open to falsification).

Hence, Critical Realism may be contrasted with 'actualism', on the one hand, and 'idealism', on the other. Actualism, though not denying the reality of events and experiences, makes no provision for the existence of underlying mechanisms, since these 'are disputed and not directly observable' (Ackroyd and Fleetwood, 2000: 6). In contrast, idealism rules out investigation of non-discursive practices in asserting that there is nothing knowable that is independent of mind, a position that is the basis of contemporary Constructionism and which has been referred to by critical realists as the 'epistemic fallacy', or the failure to separate the 'transitive' and 'intransitive' domains of social science/reality (as explained above).

'Depth' metaphors predominate in realist accounts of the natural and social worlds, thus alluding to the manner in which the multiplicity of mechanisms that conjointly provoke a given series of events and, when realised, their ensuing experiences are arranged (that is, within open systems such as nature and society as distinct from the closed system of the laboratory). In addressing this issue, Bhaskar (1978: 168–9) argues for the 'stratification of nature', that is, 'an ordered [or layered] series of mechanisms in which the lower explain without replacing the higher' (Collier, 1994: 48). Here, it is possible to distinguish between 'horizontal explanations', which 'move from the level of the happenings and phenomena to be explained to that of the mechanisms and structures which generate them' (Carter and New, 2004: 8) and 'vertical explanations', whereby one mechanism or structure is shown to be the product of another, more basic one and so on *ad infinitum*.

In the natural sciences, this process of abstraction would normally be operationalised through recourse to experimental method under laboratory conditions. However, in the social sciences closed systems cannot be established artificially, hence experiments are irrelevant; not so the 'detective-like' skills of geologists, natural historians, meteorologists and other natural scientists who study open systems (Collier, 1998). That aside, realist social science is not grounded in a particular methodology. Quantitative and qualitative methods alike may yield the empirical data from which horizontal and vertical explanations are possible.

POTENTIAL CRITICISM

There has been a distinct lack of engagement with Realism on the part of tourism scholars, aside from a few out-of-hand and not terribly helpful rejections in some introductions to tourism and social science, which, fallaciously, have a strong tendency to equate it with positivism, as discussed earlier. Most of the best critique has taken place 'in-house' in the

Journal of Critical Realism, or *Alethia* as it used to be known. Readers interested to pursue this key concept are encouraged to explore the exchange between McLennan (2009) and Benton (2009) in a recent edited collection honouring the work of Ted Benton.

CROSS REFERENCES

Figurationalism, Realism, Symbolic Interactionism.

FURTHER READING

Generic

Ackroyd, S. and Fleetwood, S. (2000) 'Realism in contemporary organisation and management studies', in S. Ackroyd and S. Fleetwood (eds), *Realist Perspectives on Management and Organisations.* London: Routledge. pp. 3–25.

Benton, T. (2004) Critical realism, in M. Lewis-Beck, R. Bryman and T.F. Liao (eds), *The SAGE Encyclopaedia of Social Science Research Methods,* Vol. 1, Thousand Oaks, CA: Sage. pp. 221–2.

Benton, T. (2009) Conclusion: philosophy, materialism and nature – comments and reflections, in S. Moog and R. Stones (eds), *Nature, Social Relations and Human Needs: Essays in Honour of Ted Benton.* Basingstoke: Palgrave Macmillan. pp. 208–43.

Bhaskar, R. (1978) *A Realist Theory of Science.* Brighton: Harvester.

Bhaskar, R. (1979) *The Possibility of Naturalism.* Hemel Hempstead: Harvester Wheatsheaf.

Carter, B. and New, C. (2004) Introduction: realist social theory and empirical research, in B. Carter and C. New (eds), *Making Realism Work: Realist Social Theory and Empirical Research.* London: Routledge. pp. 1–20.

Collier, A. (1994) *Critical Realism: An Introduction to Roy Bhaskar's Philosophy.* London: Verso.

Collier, A. (1998) Critical realism, in E. Craig (ed.), *Routledge Encyclopedia of Philosophy.* London: Routledge. URL (consulted 1 August 2003): http:www.rep.routledge.com/article/R003.

Delanty, G. (1997) *Social Science: Beyond Constructivism and Realism.* Buckingham: Open University Press.

Fleetwood, S. and Ackroyd, S. (eds) (2004) *Critical Realist Applications in Organisation and Management Studies.* London: Routledge.

Gregory, D. (1982) A realist construction of the social, *Transactions of the Institute of British Geographers* 7: 254–6.

Guba, E. (ed.) (1990) *The Paradigm Dialogue.* Newbury Park, CA: Sage.

McLennan, G. (2009) 'FOR science in the social sciences': The end of the road for Critical Realism?, in S. Moog and R. Stones (eds), *Nature, Social Relations and Human Needs: Essays in Honour of Ted Benton.* Basingstoke: Palgrave Macmillan. pp. 47–64.

critical realism

43

Sayer, A. (2001) Reply to Holmwood, *Sociology*, 35 (4): 967–84.

Sayer, A. (2004a) *Realism and Social Science*. London: Sage.

Sayer, A. (2004b) 'Why critical realism?', in S. Fleetwood and S. Ackroyd (eds), *Critical Realist Applications in Organisation and Management Studies*. London: Routledge. pp. 6–20.

Stockmann, N. (1983) *Antipositivistic Theories of the Sciences: Critical Rationalism, Critical Theory and Scientific Realism*. Dordrecht: Reidel.

Tourism specific

Botterill, D. (2003) An autoethnographic narrative on tourism research epistemologies, *Society and Leisure*, 26 (1): 97–110.

Cooper, C. (2003) Progress in tourism research, in C. Cooper (ed.), *Classic Reviews in Tourism*. Clevedon: Channel View. pp. 1–8.

Gale, T. and Botterill, D. (2005) A realist agenda for tourist studies, or why destination areas really rise and fall in popularity. *Tourist Studies*, 5 (2): 151–74.

Hollinshead, K. (2004) A primer in ontological craft, in J. Phillimore and L. Goodson (eds), *Qualitative Research in Tourism*. London: Routledge. pp. 63–82.

Jamal, T.B. and Everett, J. (2004) Resisting rationalisation in the natural and academic life-world: critical tourism research or hermeneutic charity?, *Current Issues in Tourism*, 7 (1): 1–19.

Pernecky, T. and Jamal, T. (2010) (Hermeneutic) phenomenology in tourism studies, *Annals of Tourism Research*, 37 (4): 1055–75.

Phillimore, J. and Goodson, L. (eds) (2004) *Qualitative Research in Tourism: Ontologies, Epistemologies and Methodologies*. London: Routledge.

Critical Theory

Definition Critical Theory is, at the same time, a function of social life and an autonomous theory. According to Kolakowski (1978) Critical Theory minimally meant:

1   An historical perspective on developments and contradictions in society but at the same time an independent position towards any doctrine, including Marxism.

2   The insaneness of society and the need for radical, emancipatory, change.
3   The analysis of existing society itself is part of that society and thereby requires self-reflection.

RELEVANCE

Our experience tells us that many students choose to study tourism because they want to make a difference in the world. Often an awakening occurs, or is confirmed, through the observation of the way in which tourism works in practice while on field study or on holiday, often in the less developed world where extremes of wealth and power are more obvious. If you have an aspiration to improve social and /or environmental justice through your study of tourism, then there is no better place to start than with an examination of Critical Theory. There are, of course, many implications and you should be prepared for some uncomfortable explorations of your own values and beliefs. You may find that the people you set out to 'help' are resentful of your own position in society and of your interventions. Your research project may uncover yet more dilemmas and even greater complexity than you imagined at the beginning of your study and you may be left with no simple solutions to report. These are just some of the markers of critical tourism studies inspired by Critical Theory. Undaunted, then read on ...

APPLICATION

The tourism academy settled on the legacy of Critical Theory sometime after its zenith in the social sciences in the 1960s and 1970s. It does so, therefore, carrying the currents of contemporary milieu that surrounds Critical Theory. The first of a series of four bi-annual conferences of a newly formed critical tourism studies community was held in Dubrovnik, Croatia in 2005, followed by meetings in Split in 2007, and Zadar in 2009. A fourth meeting is planned for Cardiff in the summer of 2011.

An edited collection provides evidence of the influence of Critical Theory at the first conference (Ateljevic et al., 2008). Reflexivity and the relations between the social researcher and the social world were highlighted in many papers. Critical arguments against the current forms of tourism were mounted by invoking proposals that went beyond the business logics of tourism management. Methodologies were applied in a

criticalist manner with examples from Grounded Theory, Constructionism, Ethnomethodology, diary and memory-work from Feminism, oral
history and lifecourse analysis. These legacies of Critical Theory were
positioned alongside newer streams of thought such as Postmodernism,
post-structuralism, deconstructionism and Post-colonialism despite the
often serious points of difference between them and mainstream 'Frankfurt
School' thinking that initially inspired Critical Theory.

The eclectic mix within the critical tourism studies community also
reflects another legacy of Critical Theory as, despite the singular force
suggested by its label, from its beginning in 1923 there were many differences between the major protagonists of Critical Theory. Nevertheless, it
is possible to pick out echoes of Critical Theory in the research of critical
tourism scholars. A critique of ideological influence in, for examples, the
neo-liberalism within tourism education and gender power in tourism
advertising, is inspired by the requirement of Critical Theory of an imma-
nent (permanently pervading) encounter with the existing social order.

The idea of social movements as vehicles for change and experimentation is captured in the work on 'voluntourism' and alternative tourism
and provides space for the transcendent possibility and utopian ideals of
latter-day critical theorists. However, such small-scale explorations
would never satisfy Critical Theory's insistence on a radical change that
would confront and overturn injustice in world tourism.

The third gathering of critical tourism scholars in Zadar in 2009 took
'critical pedagogy' as its focus. The attempt here was to engage in a reflexive
analysis of the material conditions in which tourism knowledge is advanced.
As an example, focus at the conference was placed on the regimes of quality assessment in teaching and research in university life and the systems of
surveillance and control that potentially damage and constrain the pursuit
of learning. Other themes in tourism studies that are influenced by a critical
tradition are the commodification of tourism and leisure and the struggle
for emancipation in a wide range of peoples, located in many parts of the
world, who are damaged by or excluded from tourism.

Following Habermas' *Theory of Communicative Action* (1984) we can
locate these interests of tourism researchers in the collisions between
the imperatives of the economic and political system and the communicative structures of the life-world.

The influence of Habermas' notion of the 'colonisation of the life-
world by the system' has to some degree been replaced by Foucault's
'genealogical analysis of anonymous power' in studies of the tourism
system. However, the intention under both approaches is to expose

key concepts in
tourism research

regimes of 'truth'. The replacement of the meta-narrative with a plethora of previously silent voices is a hallmark of the practices of the critical tourism collective (see, for example, Wijesinghe and Willis, 2010).

HISTORICAL DEVELOPMENT

It would be impossible to fully understand Critical Theory without considering the historical and political conditions that created it in the early 1920s. The Institute for Social Research was formed in Frankfurt in 1923 by social scientists unhappy about the situation in Germany's political left. They did not approve of what they considered an anti-socialist attitude of the social democrats (SPD) but neither did they trust the Moscow dependency of their communist counterparts (KPD). Instead these unsatisfactory political practices led them to form an independent centre for the development of social theory, known as the Frankfurt School. Independence was understood to be 'a necessary prerequisite for theoretical innovation and unrestrained social research' (Jay, 1973: 5) and proved particularly important given the rigid climate in German universities during the 1920s and 1930s that worsened under the grip of National Socialism.

Until 1930 the Frankfurt School had pursued a neo-Marxist political economy project mainly in the area of the workers' movement. In 1930 Max Horkheimer was appointed its leader and he introduced the new project of Critical Theory in his writings in the Institute's *Journal of Social Research*. In proposing a new project that would fuse philosophy with empirical social science Horkheimer never lost sight of the situating of social phenomena within an historical context, as well as an awareness of philosophy's role in shaping the very society it sought to discover. Under his leadership he attracted many new adherents and the scope of his project drifted away from orthodox Marxism to embrace a growing interest in psycho-analysis and a more dialectical, neo-Hegelian materialism. Following the Nazi assumption of power in 1933, the Institute moved away from Frankfurt, first to Geneva and then after a short time in Paris to the centre of the capitalist world, New York.

During the1930s the proponents of Critical Theory became pessimistic about the possibilities of creating a more rational and happy society. The improved material conditions in advanced societies and the growing consumption of, and influence of, mass-culture on the proletariat seemed destined to undermine the historical roll of a revolutionary working class movement. The Institute instead turned its attention to understanding the disappearance of the 'negative' critical forces in the world. In the USA critical theorists concentrated on the structure and development of authority and the massive influence of the culture industry. The research teams at the Institute integrated psycho-analysis into its theoretical framework and did empirical studies on Nazism and anti-Semitism with a culminating point being the publication of 'Studies in Prejudice' and 'The Authoritarian Personality'. These studies were undertaken with their American colleagues among who Paul Lazarsfeld was the most influential.

During this empirical period the resident American researchers attempted to stop the publication of output in German. The European members of the Institute resisted this argument by stressing the importance of defending a threatened humanist tradition in a Germany besieged by Nazism. The next project was the development of an aesthetic theory and a critique of mass culture. 'Dialectic der Aufklärung' (1947) or 'Dialectic of Enlightenment' by Horkheimer and Adorno became probably the Institute's most important theoretical source of inspiration. It had been written in the light of the Jewish genocide in Europe, which, almost certainly, had highly influenced its pessimism. Later it became the inspiration again during the rebellion against the consumer society in the 1960s and again during the rise of Postmodernism and its critique of symbolic consumption.

The influential intellectual project of Juergen Habermas was rooted in the Frankfurt School but later he turned away from some of the basic assumptions of Critical Theory to create a less radical form. The trajectory of radical withdrawal is captured by changes to the nicknames of the Frankfurt School. Before the Second World War the Institute had been named the Cafe Marx, because of its hospitality to many non-orthodox Marxists. After the war it changed into Cafe Max, because of the influence of Max Horkheimer and because the loss of the 'r' symbolised the perceived loss of radicalism. Since Habermas became the most important representative of Critical Theory its Marxist origins definitely came to an end. These changes led Kolakowski (1978) to the view that they were symptomatic of the breakdown of this system of thought in general.

DESCRIPTION

Critical Theory reacted against the analytical-empirical, positivist tradition in the social sciences. It asserted that disinterested scientific research was impossible in a society that is in need of change. Critical Theory rests on four main foundations. First, a self-reflective approach by the researcher towards the object of study related, second, to the social-scientific contribution to emancipation or the elimination of cruel and repressive practices through what has been called 'correct praxis' in which free and really rational theory and practice are unified. The third foundation is related to the critique of Webber's value-free science: Critical Theory disputes the fact–value separation, incorporates values, opinions, cultural convictions and experiences that various groups of people share. The role of Critical Theory is to find a normative position between these many voices. The fourth foundation is related to the acquisition of empirical knowledge that, although appearing to adopt the methods of a positivist science, did so only in the understanding that such process was surrounded by the other three foundations.

POTENTIAL CRITICISM

A theory that is both of and in society will be subject to the shifting changes within society. It is, and never was, a fixed entity. A critique of Critical Theory becomes more an examination of how it changes. This is exactly how Habermas has operated. He has sought to move Critical Theory on in anticipation of the direction of societal change. Critical researchers continue to be inspired by Critical Theory. They call current ideology into question and initiate action in the cause of greater social justice. Typically this involves them in interrogating commonly held values and assumptions, challenging conventional social structures and engaging in social action. The extent to which these practices can find some form of expression and spaces in which to operate is not just a function of the balance of conservative and radical mores of the time but it is also in the vibrancy and relevance of current Critical Theory. In this sense the critique of Critical Theory comes as much from within its ranks as it is inspired by any external, competing thesis (see, for example, Bronner, 1994: 321–52).

CROSS REFERENCES

Critical Realism, Ethnomethodology, Hermeneutics.

critical theory

FURTHER READING

Generic

Bronner, S.E. (1994) *Of Critical Theory and its Theorists*. Oxford: Blackwell.
Habermas, J. (1984) *The Theory of Communicative Action*, trans. T. McCarthy. Cambridge: Polity.

Jay, M. (1973) *The Dialectical Imagination*. Boston, MA: Little Brown and Co.

Kolakowski, L. (1978) *Main Currents of Marxism: Its Origins, Growth and Dissolution*. Oxford: Oxford University Press.

Tourism specific

Ateljevic, I., Pritchard, A. and Morgan, N. (eds) (2008) *The Critical Turn in Tourism Studies: Innovative Research Methodologies*. Oxford: Elsevier.

Wijesinghe, G. and Willis, P. (2010) Receiving and shaping the tourist appraising gaze: the lived experience of reception work in the tourism and hospitality industry, in P.M. Burns, J.M. Lester and L. Bibbings (eds), *Tourism and Visual Culture, Volume 1: Theories and Concepts*. Wallingford: CABI. pp. 150–64.

Deduction

Definition To conclude predictions about individual experiences from general statements, hypotheses or theories about regularities in nature or society.

RELEVANCE

The relative lack of distinctive theory would seem to limit the usefulness of this key concept entry to student research projects in tourism, however, it is very much recommended that if you are working in a social sciences context such as business and management studies, economics or psychology then you should carefully work through the arguments below. Why? Well, Deduction is the basis of knowledge production in the natural sciences and for many in the social sciences it offers the purest route to new knowledge, even if its translation from the natural to the social world is fraught with difficulties. It is likely that your research methods training will be based upon the nomological (that is law-like) deductive process of science and even if you decide to reject it as a way of researching in your own project, you should understand it fully and know why you have made alternative choices. If you are working from the setting of an academic discipline such as economics or psychology (and some traditions in sociology and geography) then you will have a larger body of theory from which to develop a research project in tourism studies using Deduction.

APPLICATION

According to the normative practices of tourism research training and the typical guide to doing research in tourism (see, for example, Smith, 2010) we might conclude that this type of research dominates the field. Research methods books and teaching and learning about research, often delivered by non-tourism specialists, seems to suggest that nomothetic (law like), deductive research is a highly desirable practice in tourism research. The question for us is whether this is true or indeed desirable at this stage in the development of tourism knowledge. We tend to agree with McKercher (2009) who argues that hypothesis testing is often simply inappropriate and produces an undesirable, conservative tendency in students' research.

In most tourism research, as in much social scientific research, academics do not work within a tradition of deducing hypotheses to be tested from general theories. If they do, then they tend to borrow theory from disciplines or other fields of study. A typical example would be Park and Stowkowski's (2009) use of social disruption theory in their study of crime in rural communities. The borrowing of theory from other disciplines is a function of the very few theories specific to tourism knowledge, an exception being Butler's resort life-cycle theory (see Gale and Botterill [2005] as an example of theory development in tourism). The situation in tourism research is therefore very different from the natural sciences, where deductive practices dominate and where thoroughly tested theories are constantly in the process of refinement and testing.

Instead, we would argue that the normative practice of tourism researchers is to treat empirical generalisations as scientific, even where there is no relationship to any theory. This procedure can be better characterised as inductive rather than deductive. Gradually, one hopes to come from different empirical generalisations to generalisations that hold for more than just a single situation. Sometimes, theories are used in tourism research but without the intention to test them. The relationship between theory and data in tourism research is thus somewhat different from that found within nomothetic, deductive research.

Smith and Lee (2010) have surveyed the tourism literature to produce an analysis of the use of the term theory. They construct seven types of the use of the term theory. Their analysis confirms the very limited adoption of nomological deductive research (Type 1 in their classification) and recent growth of the use of the term theory in what they describe as a largely meaningless way (Type 7). In an attempt to regain the ground for deduction in tourism research they conclude, 'Still, we suggest that "theory", in a published research context, should be limited to Type 1 and Type 2 theory. In other words, "theory" is most appropriately used in the context of models that are based on substantial empirical evidence and that produce falsifiable predictions' (Smith and Lee, 2010: 11). In support of the assertion of Smith and Lee, Jenkins (2009) provides a valiant defence of hypo-deductive research in tourism and makes his own suggestions for corrections in its current misuse.

HISTORICAL DEVELOPMENT

The image of science has long been dominated by the induction-principle. From individual statements about various experiences one is thought to be able to formulate general statements about laws of nature (= induction). If this principle were correct it is possible that what we have observed in the past and continue to observe in the present, we will also observe in the future. When there has always been a relationship between two phenomena X and Y, this will remain the case in the future, then and only then can we formulate predictions with certainty. In other words, the induction-principle guarantees a certain foundation for scientific predictions. Using this principle, empirical testing of individual statements produces firm conclusions from which scientific laws may be established.

It was the 18th-century philosopher Hume (1906) who first attacked the induction-principle. According to him there can never be any certainty about the future, based on the past and present. We will never be sure about the truth of our theories. Every theory is falsifiable. Sir Karl Raymund Popper (1974), probably the most important philosopher in modern times, who's ideas have shaped contemporary nomological deductive research, began his own reasoning from Hume's falsification of the induction-principle. Importantly, Popper concluded that there is no criterion of truth, and any certainty about the truth is impossible.

Having had numerous articles published in 'positivist' scientific journals in his lifetime, Popper was considered by many to be a positivist. His rejection of any truth criterion, however, spawned his later opposition to Positivism. Popper's argument was as follows. For a convinced positivist, truth equals meaningfulness, equals science. Everything that cannot be tested scientifically is meaningless and not true. Popper, to the contrary, distinguishes between science and truth. We can never be certain about the truth, he asserts. Therefore, a criterion of truth does not exist. However, a criterion for science does. Science can be distinguished from non-science by starting with the opposite of the quest for certainty. We can never establish any certainty Popper argued, but we should rejoice in the refutation of our own hypotheses. Only when a hypothesis can be refuted in principle, can it be called scientific.

In this image of what science is, induction has become unnecessary. The route to scientific knowledge is the other way round, which implies Deduction. We should not move from perceptions to theory. Rather, the starting point should be the production of bold hypotheses, built upon earlier tested (disproven or not) hypotheses. New hypotheses are tested as before by trying to disprove them as vigorously as possible. In this way science reveals reality on an ever deeper level. After each refutation, new possible hypotheses need to be conjectured, deduced from general theories, thus science becomes an exciting adventure, during a process in which new hypotheses are conjectured with an ever stronger explanatory power. Popper pleads for a healthy climate of continuous (self-) criticism; the bigger the mistake, the bigger the possible improvement. Theories should not systematically try to avoid refutations – as in Freudianism or in large parts of Marxism, of which some parts have now been refuted by history – but open themselves up to criticism.

Popper's position is one of a naive falsificationist. The law of the 'excluded contradiction' (A cannot be equal to non-A) remains the guideline for the scientific method. In science each subsequent contradiction has a consequence for the general, theoretical background. Methodologically this falsificationism becomes more nuanced and sophisticated. Direct refutations of hypotheses are rare exceptions. When they occur they are crucial, of course. Even more importantly, who decides whether a hypothesis has been refuted? According to Popper, only the academic community can take this decision against the background of the scientific knowledge of that particular moment. Therefore, in practice it appears not to be that easy to refute a hypothesis. However, the falsifiability of hypotheses in light of the existing theories remains important as a guideline for a scientific method. As a result of this criterion, science can be distinguished from other forms of knowledge and therefore deduction becomes the rule of science. Different theories compete with one another by being tested in the most trenchant possible manner, i.e. falsifiability. New theories include the older ones and add explanatory power to them. In this way, it is claimed, we will approach the truth more closely by eliminating the untruth, without ever being sure of the truth.

DESCRIPTION

Deduction starts from a thoroughly tested background body of theories. From these theories hypotheses can be deduced to be tested. Thus, deduction goes from general to specific. For example, in Durkheim's (2006) theory of suicide, there is a general theory that assumes a relationship between suicide and social cohesion leading to the hypothesis that the bigger the social cohesion in a group, the smaller the chance of suicide among its members. If it has been demonstrated that social cohesion is stronger among Catholics than among Protestants, then the hypothesis is that the incidence of suicide is higher among Protestants than Catholics. The last steps, then, consist of developing the best possible conditions and empirical circumstances in which this hypothesis can be tested, interpreted again and new hypotheses can be formulated on the basis of these interpretations.

Methodology plays its crucial role in (social) scientific research. It provides us with guidelines about how to formulate hypotheses, how to test and reinterpret them and then how to arrive at new hypotheses. This last (and first) phase has been called the hypothesis-generating phase and what happens afterwards has been called the hypothesis-testing phase. Often this first phase has been compared with a combination of deduction and induction and the second phase with deduction. Therefore only during the second phase would Popper's criterion be valid, because it is at this point through testing that the strongest possible criticism would be implemented. In the first phase, which requires freedom of design, much more arbitrariness is allowed.

POTENTIAL CRITICISM

Criticism of Deduction must start with an alternative view of how science produces knowledge that was developed by Thomas Kuhn. While Popper was arguing for a unifying and universal definition of scientific knowledge, Kuhn sought to show how science progressed through periods of normal and abnormal science shaped not by any internal criteria of science but by wider social and cultural conditions. We explain Kuhn's approach in the key concept entry for Paradigm. His arguments would suggest that even if Popper's falsification thesis has become the norm in the natural sciences at this point in time there is always a possibility of it being superseded during a period of revolutionary, abnormal scientific activity. His argument rests on studying the cultural and social practices of science and argued that wider contexts in which science occurs are more powerful in shaping scientific knowledge production than internal criteria such as falsification

A second point of criticism arises from the translation of the deductive approach from the natural to the social sciences. If Deduction is the only route to scientific knowledge, then where we might ask is the deductive research in the social sciences and, by extension, in tourism research? The problem for the social sciences to overcome, if they are to emulate the natural sciences and adopt Popperian falsification as the basis for the production of scientific knowledge, is the current cleavage between theory development and empirical research that accompanies social scientific endeavour. Theoretical development often takes place without empirical testing and in a parallel process empirical research takes place outside of theoretical development. Deduction in the social sciences becomes a huge if not impossible task in this context and inductive research appears to be the only possible route. Bridging this divide has been seriously attempted in very few areas of social science, for example in psychophysiology and in econometrics but as our reading of Smith and Lee (2010) suggests this aspiration is still very much alive and well for some tourism researchers.

The third point of critique emerges from the challenge of the interpretive tradition in the social sciences that is informed not by natural science but by research traditions in the humanities. The core task for social scientists under interpretivism is to understand the meaning that people attribute to various realities of which they are a part. Deduction plays hardly any role in this opposing tradition, where a more qualitative methodology prevails. Dilthey (1976) captured this dispute in his claim that there are two traditions of science, one (explanatory) in the *Naturwissenschaften* and one (interpretive) in the *Geisteswissenschaften*. Most social scientists today, however, seem to agree upon the necessity to combine the two traditions in some way or another. There is still much disagreement on how to accomplish this, but the fact that they should be combined is more and more accepted within contemporary social science.

deduction

CROSS REFERENCES

Empiricism, Modelling, Positivism.

FURTHER READING

Generic

Dilthey, W. (1976) *Selected Writings*. Cambridge: Cambridge University Press.
Durkheim, E. (2006) *On Suicide*. London: Penguin Books.
Hume, D. (1906) *Hume's Essays*. London: Watts.
Kuhn, T. (1962) *The Structure of Scientific Revolution*. Chicago, IL: University of Chicago Press.
Popper, K. (1974) *The Philosophy of Karl Popper*. La Salle, IL: Open Court.

Tourism specific

Gale, T. and Botterill, D. (2005) A realist agenda for tourist studies, or why destination areas really rise and fall in popularity. *Tourist Studies*, 5 (2): 151–74.
Jenkins, C.L. (2009) Unravelling myths in tourism research, *Tourism Recreation Research*, 34 (3): 319–23.
McKercher, B. (2009) Research conservatism is responsible for myths in tourism research, *Tourism Recreation Research*, 34 (3): 324–5.
Park, M.K. and Stokowski, P.A. (2009) Social disruption theory and crime in rural communities: comparisons across three levels of tourism growth, *Tourism Management*, 30 (6): 905–15.
Smith, S. (2010) *Practical Tourism Research*. Wallingford: CABI.
Smith, S. and Lee, H. (2010) A typology of 'theory' in tourism, in D. Pearce and R. Butler (eds), *Tourism Research: A 20–20 Vision*. Oxford: Goodfellow Publishers. pp. 28–42.

Delphi Method

Definition The Delphi Method is a structured process for collecting and distilling knowledge from a group of experts by means of rounds of data collection interspersed with selective feedback.

RELEVANCE

If you are seeking to garner opinion about an aspect of tourism, its quality management processes for example, then the Delphi Method is a relevant key concept to consider. The topic of research has to be of interest to the expert panel members and its outcomes should add value to the experts' own knowledge and not just provide you with a dissertation or thesis. So you'll have to be on top of your subject and very well read in the research literature in order to know what questions to ask of your experts. The critical factor in selecting the Delphi Method is whether your project will last long enough to both establish an expert panel and undertake several rounds of opinion data and feedback. Even if you are a very well organised researcher and have the help of your supervisor to recruit experts to your panel, then a 12-month minimum period is needed. Communication between yourself and the members of the expert panel is vital to success. All aspects of the research must be delivered on time and be professional in all respects if you want to ensure their continued commitment to the research project.

APPLICATION

The Delphi Method has been applied in two ways to address several topics within tourism research. In its classic role as a forecasting tool it has been applied to the uptake of innovations in mobile technology (Katsura and Sheldon, 2008) and information technology in hotel management (Singh and Kasavana, 2005). It has also been used as a comparative qualitative forecasting technique to quantitative approaches in economic impact assessment, for example, in South Australia (Tideswell et al., 2001), and for calculating visitor volume estimates for a major event in Korea (Lee et al., 2008).

Deviating from its forecasting origins, the method has also been used as a tool for garnering expert opinion in a number of controversial areas of tourism research. This is particularly so in the thorny matter of stakeholders' opinions around sustainable, nature-based and rural tourism planning and development. Typically these studies seek to establish expert consensus on a range of indicators that might be used in evaluating development and management practices (see, for example, Spenceley [2008] on nature-based tourism in Southern Africa and Choi and Sirikaya [2006] on community involvement). In a sophisticated application of the Delphi Method, Briedenhann (2007) combines data collected through interviews, focus groups and four rounds of a Delphi study to examine the role of the pubic sector in rural tourism development. Finally, the method has found favour with tourism researchers exploring destination competitiveness in Croatia (Kaynak and Cavlek, 2006), Tiawan (Lee and King, 2006) and Botswana (Kaynak and Marandu, 2006).

delphi method

The name 'Delphi' originates from ancient Greece where it was the location of one of most important shrines in all Greece. Built around a sacred spring, Delphi was considered to be the *omphalos* – the centre (literally the navel) of the world. The shrine was visited by those seeking to have questions about the future answered by Pythia, the priestess of Apollo.

The contemporary use of the term in the social sciences refers to a forecasting method developed as part of a corporate research and development strategy for the application of new technology in the military in the 1940s. The Delphi Method recognises human judgement as legitimate and useful inputs in generating forecasts but the problem the method sought to overcome was how to use this testimony and, specifically, how to combine the testimony of a number of experts into a single useful statement.

The first commercial Delphi applications were in the area of technological forecasting and aimed to forecast likely inventions, new technologies and the social and economic impact of technological change (Adler and Ziglio, 1996). Delphi has subsequently found its way into industry, government, and universities. It has simultaneously expanded beyond technological forecasting into public health, education and, as is evidenced above, tourism. A recent search in the Social Sciences Citation Index and the Science Citation Index demonstrates the growth in popularity of the method with 65 relevant items; 1 from the 1960s, 8 from the 1970s, 3 from the 1980s, 21 from the 1990s and 32 up to 2007 (Green et al., 2007).

DESCRIPTION

The Delphi Method enables discussion between experts without permitting certain social interactive behaviour that may hamper opinion forming. For the researcher it is an exercise in group communication among a panel of geographically dispersed experts (Adler and Ziglio, 1996). The essence of the technique is fairly straightforward. It comprises a series of questionnaires sent either by post or email (for which there are some dedicated software packages available, see, for example, http://www.forecasting principles.com) to a pre-selected group of experts. The questionnaires are designed to elicit and develop individual responses to the problems posed and to enable the experts to refine their views as the group's work progresses in accordance with the assigned task and the feedback provided. Fowles (1978) describes 10 steps in the Delphi Method:

1   Formation of a team to undertake and monitor a Delphi on a given subject.

2 Selection of one or more panels to participate in the exercise. Customarily, the panellists are experts in the area to be investigated.
3 Development of the first round Delphi questionnaire.
4 Testing the questionnaire for proper wording (e.g. ambiguities, vagueness).
5 Transmission of the first questionnaires to the panellists.
6 Analysis of the first round responses.
7 Preparation of the second round questionnaires (and possible testing).
8 Transmission of the second round questionnaires to the panellists.
9 Analysis of the second round responses (Steps 7 to 9 are reiterated as long as desired or necessary to achieve stability in the results usually not more than four times).
10 Preparation of a report by the analysis team to present the conclusions of the exercise.

POTENTIAL CRITICISM

Clearly of critical importance to the validity of the findings is the quality of the expertise in the panel. The process is liable to what has been called 'the simplification urge' as experts tend to judge the future of events in isolation from other developments. The process does require a high level of commitment from the respondents and there is always the possibility of fatigue and drop-out among the expert panel. The role of the monitor, or researcher, who provides selective feedback is also a perceived weakness and to counter this it is recommended that selection criteria are consistent throughout the duration of the study.

CROSS REFERENCES

Constructionism.

FURTHER READING

Generic

Adler, M. and Ziglio E. (eds) (1996) *Gazing into the Oracle: The Delphi Method and its Application to Social Policy and Public Health*. London: Jessica Kingsley Publishers.
Fowles, J. (1978) *Handbook of Futures Research*. Westport, CT: Greenwood Press.
Green, K.C., Armstrong, S.J. and Graefe, A. (2007) Methods to elicit forecasts from groups: Delphi and prediction markets compared. URL (accessed April 2009): http://mpra.ub.uni-muenchen.de/4999/

delphi method

Tourism specific

Briedenhann, J. (2007) The role of the public sector in rural tourism: respondents' views, *Current Issues in Tourism*, 10 (6): 584–607.

Choi, H.S. and Sirakaya, E. (2006) Sustainability indicators for managing community tourism, *Tourism Management*, 27 (6): 1274–89.

Kaynak, E. and Cavlek, N. (2006) Measurement of tourism market potential of Croatia by use of Delphi qualitative research technique, *Journal of East-West Business*, 12 (4): 105–23.

Kaynak, E. and Marandu, E. (2006) Tourism market potential analysis in Botswana: a Delphi study, *Journal of Travel Research*, 45 (2): 227–37.

Katsura, T. and Sheldon, P. (2008) Forecasting mobile technology use in Japanese tourism, *Information Technology & Tourism*, 10 (3): 201–14.

Lee, C.-F. and King, B. (2006) Assessing destination competitiveness: an application to the hot springs tourism sector, *Tourism and Hospitality: Planning & Development*, 3 (3): 179–97.

Lee, C.-K., Song, H.-J. and Mjelde, J.W. (2008) The forecasting of international expo tourism using quantitative and qualitative techniques, *Tourism Management*, 29 (6): 1084–98.

Singh, A.J. and Kasavana, M.L. (2005) The impact of information technology on future management of lodging operations: a Delphi study to predict key technological events in 2007 and 2027, *Tourism and Hospitality Research*, 6 (1): 24–37.

Spenceley, A. (2008) Requirements for sustainable nature-based tourism in transfrontier conservation areas: a Southern African Delphi consultation, *Tourism Geographies*, 10 (3): 285–311.

Tideswell, C., Mules, T. and Faulkner, B. (2001) An integrative approach to tourism forecasting: a glance in the rearview mirror, *Journal of Travel Research*, 40 (2): 162.

Document Analysis

Definition The exploration of the social world through physical, embodied text wherein text can take many forms: written, audio, visual and electronic.

RELEVANCE

Document Analysis is a hidden gem of social research that is often ignored as a key concept for research projects conducted by tourism students whose idea about 'doing' research is to get out into the field and collect data. It can either support a complete research project in its own right or can usefully provide a source of evidence in a case study and provide supplementary data to a survey or interviews. Remember it has a singular advantage over other ways of working in that documents are always 'there', you will not be dependent on being able to get to your case study location, having the right weather for survey work, or persuading respondents to find the space and time in their diaries to meet with you. As for all key concepts it makes specific demands on your time and effort. It requires a great deal of patience to sort through hundreds of pages of text; a comfortable chair and a large desk are to be recommended. The occasional spring clean of the desk might be a good idea, too, to avoid any health and safety hazards from the build up of debris from snacks, lunches and dinners taken while working, get the picture! It also requires an innate love of reading, a preference for your own company, and a forensic-like inquiring mind to track down documents and search through material for connecting strands of argument, or as they have become better known, discourses.

APPLICATION

Interest in Document Analysis among tourism researches has largely followed its general fortune in social science since the 1950s (see below). Consequently, Document Analysis was, until fairly recently, the singular preserve of a very few social historians and historical geographers who conduct tourism research, for example Walton's (2000, 2007) studies of British seaside resorts and Towner and Page (1996) in their ambitious study of the history of tourism and recreation.

Hannam and Knox (2005) refer to a recent growth in the use of documents in tourism research. Documents are often analysed as a component of multi-method approaches to research problems. For example, Kasim (2007) incorporates qualitative data obtained via elite interviewing, document analysis and personal observation in order to discuss the theoretical drivers of, and barriers to, corporate environmentalism in the hotel sector in Malaysia. Furthermore, Strange and Kempa (2003) draw upon policy documents, onsite observations, tourist surveys and interviews to explore how former sites of punishment and incarceration have become a popular tourist experience when defunct prisons are converted into museums or heritage sites.

Documents have also become the basis for policy analysis in tourism planning, see for examples Fennel and Ebert (2004) on the consequences of the precautionary principle for tourism development and Hyslop and Eagles (2007) on the creation of an ideal framework for visitor management in North American national parks, national wildlife areas and refuges. The Ayikoru et al. (2009) study of tourism education in English universities is informed by documents selected to represent the period 1960–2004 and drawn from both private archives and published government sources.

HISTORICAL DEVELOPMENT

The development of document analysis in the social sciences is closely linked with the development of technologies that communicate text. McCulloch (2004) argues that social scientists facing increasing social complexity in the 20th century began to look for more ways to capture social evidence. Recognition that vast archives of documents were being created in both the public and private domains of life led to the possibility that such records might provide insights into the workings of social process and social structure. Governments busily recorded their responses to social problems and issues in a mountain of official documents. Technologies of the printed word combined with transport infrastructure created wider and faster distribution of newspapers and magazines. Levels of literacy were increasing, thus enabling individuals to record their own responses to the opportunities and challenges of early 20th century life through diary accounts, letters and postcards.

In the social science academy, a landmark study, 'The Polish Peasant in Europe and America' undertaken between 1918/20 and 1927, drew heavily on both the private letters of émigrés to America and public records of the social institutions that were created to receive the new migrant workforce. The study had a tremendous influence on sociology and similar approaches to other social issues were encouraged by the Chicago School of Sociology. The work of Helen and Robert Lynd, published in 1929, documenting so called middletown American life is typical of the period in using multiple sources of document and text.

Reactions against document analysis, particularly in the 1950s, resulted in a preference for both small- and large-scale social surveys and the techniques of interviewing, observation and questionnaires began to marginalise the importance of documents in social research. Document research, it was claimed, related to the past, only reflected the views of the elite, and was an inefficient and error strewn way for social scientists to capture contemporary society.

Despite the continuing lack of recognition of document analysis in mainstream social science there is now a growing interest in the use of documents in studies inspired by Plummer's publication of the 'Documents of Life' (first in 1981 and a revised edition in 2001). His espousal of critical humanism is still controversial but in documenting the rise in interest in the biographical, the narrative and life story, Plummer has reasserted the value of document analysis. In conjunction with new communications technologies and electronic storage, the prospects for documents to provide connections between individuals and society are driving a renewed interest in them across the social sciences.

Document analysis does not carry any strong philosophical commitments. Rather it has been associated with some specific, and rejected by other, methodological communities (McCulloch, 2004). For example in the 1930s it was closely associated with sociological interactionism and as is described above was rejected in favour of the positivist turn to social research methods that lent themselves to quantification in the social sciences in the 1960s. More recently it has provided the preferred method of those concerned to de-centre and de-colonise intellectual life, enabling multiple life stories to be heard and subsequently to challenge the alleged narrow white, Anglo-centric, able bodied and male narrative of Western humanism.

DESCRIPTION

Authorship is a principal concern in Document Analysis. Authorship may be personal and identifiable or anonymous and collective expressions of the public sphere. Public sphere documents derive from both state sources and private bureaucracies. Documents can also be classified by their accessibility. From those that are open to only a very few and usually heavily vetted researchers, to openly published documents or those held in open archives. These characteristics of documents are not just a matter of fact but are crucial to the researcher in assessing their quality on four criteria: authenticity; credibility; representativeness; and meaning (Scott, 2004).

Of all of these criteria, 'meaning' is the most difficult to handle. Working on documents requires what Rapley (2007: 113) calls 'reading against and with the grain of a text'. Exploring a text depends as much on focusing on what is not said – the silence gaps and omissions – as what is said or included. Analysis of documents can incorporate simple Content Analysis or it may, dependent on the theoretical interpretation, be more concerned with how elements of a text are combined to consolidate (or disrupt) meanings. This is certainly true of critical tourism research and in their discussion of critical discourse analysis Hannam and Knox (2005) urge tourism researchers to consider more carefully the theoretical orientations that surround document and textual analysis:

> Increasing numbers of researchers in the field of tourism studies are using discourse analysis as a means of critical investigation when faced with qualitative or textual forms of data, such as written documents, or visual materials such as photographs and brochures. Such data is often representative of how a group of people have made sense of and reflected on their own world and that of others. However, there are many different types of discourse analysis and many different ways in which discourse analysis has been deployed ... It is also argued that it is important to note the interruptions and disruptions that occur within the flow of qualitative data. Utilising discourse analysis should mean the development of a more nuanced reading of the data and thus add a more critical edge to much tourism research. (Hannam and Knox, 2005: 23)

POTENTIAL CRITICISM

Criticisms of Document Analysis fall squarely into the vexed question of the theoretical and philosophical stance of the researcher. As reported above, the rejection of document analysis in the mid-20th century as a means for social research was inspired by the turn to positivism and quantification in the social sciences. This move, in turn, has been challenged by Constructionism and this has re-stimulated interest in documents in many forms and deconstructionists take the argument further by insisting that humans are simply 'fictional subjectivities found in discourse, regimes of truth and technologies of self' (Plummer, 2001: 256).

CROSS REFERENCES

Constructionism, Content Analysis, Narrative, Postmodernism.

FURTHER READING

Generic

McCulloch, G. (2004) *Documentary Research in Education, History and the Social Sciences*. London: RoutledgeFalmer.
Plummer, K. (2001) *Documents of Life 2: An Invitation to Critical Humanism*. London: Sage.

Rapley, T. (2007) *Doing Conversation, Discourse and Document Analysis.* London: Sage.

Scott, J. (2004) Documents, in M. Lewis-Beck, R. Bryman and T.F. Liao (eds), *The SAGE Encyclopaedia of Social Science Research Methods*, Vol. 1. Thousand Oaks, CA: Sage. pp. 281–4.

Tourism specific

Ayikoru, M., Tribe, J. and Airey, D (2009) Reading tourism education: neoliberalism unveiled, *Annals of Tourism Research*, 36 (2): 191–222.

Fennel, D.A. and Ebert, K. (2004) Tourism and the precautionary principle, *Journal of Sustainable Tourism*, 12 (6): 461–79.

Hannam, K. and Knox, D. (2005) Discourse analysis in tourism research: a critical perspective, *Tourism Recreation Research*, 30 (2): 23–30.

Hyslop, K.E. and Eagles, P.E.J. (2007) Visitor management policy of national parks, national wildlife areas and refuges in Canada and the United States: a policy analysis of public documents, *Leisure/Loisir*, 31 (2): 475–99.

Kasim, A. (2007) Corporate environmentalism in the hotel sector: evidence of drivers and barriers in Penang, Malaysia, *Journal of Sustainable Tourism*, 15 (6): 680–99.

Strange, C. and Kempa, M. (2003) Shades of dark tourism: Alcatraz and Robben Island, *Annals of Tourism Research*, 30 (2): 386–405.

Towner, J. and Page, S.J. (1996) *An Historical Geography of Recreation and Tourism in the Western World 1540–1940.* Chichester: Wiley.

Walton, J. (2000) *The British Seaside: Holiday and Resorts in the Twentieth Century.* Manchester: Manchester University Press.

Walton, J. (2007) *Riding on Rainbows: Blackpool Pleasure Beach and its Place in British Popular Culture.* St Albans: Skelter Publishing.

.... Empiricism ....

Definition A philosophical position in which all knowledge of existence must be justified by experience through sense data.

RELEVANCE

Quite simply you wouldn't be doing a research project at all if it were not for Empiricism, read on …

APPLICATION

Despite the negative connotations that are associated with Empiricism in the social sciences today (Hammersley, 2004) both the term 'empirical' and an appeal to 'experience' are commonplace in tourism studies. A dependence upon the idea of scientific progress through the collection of empirical evidence remains central to the vast majority of published tourism research output (see Deduction). This is reinforced by the criteria of scientific excellence that are used to judge the quality of research output across the academy. How can this be?

To answer this question then we need to acknowledge the particular and enduring influences of some social science disciplines – economics, psychology and functionalist sociology – to tourism studies. Contributors from these disciplinary camps have shaped the nature of scholarship in tourism studies and more importantly have informed the formation of the fields of marketing, particular consumer psychology, and management studies. Both marketing and management studies are highly influential within orthodox tourism research. It is also these same social science disciplines and two fields of study that are the most enthusiastic about advancing knowledge empirically in the social sciences, and with a few exceptions, quantitatively. Consequentially, tourism studies continues to be enthusiastically, and some would argue uncritically, empirical.

It is clear that the contemporary brand of Empiricism in evidence in the tourism research literature is far removed from its radical, classical form. However it remains true to the insistence on the primacy of sense data and for a method inspired by science. For example, a database search for references to 'tourism' and 'empirical' in the abstract field of Leisuretourism.com between 2000–2009 results in over 600 citations. In the majority of these studies the authors' use of the term 'empirical' refers solely to the method of collection of primary data.

In other sections of this book (see Cross References below) we account for some of the advancement of Empiricism from its early classical form of inquiry in the natural sciences, to the form of logical positivism that was dominant in the social sciences in the mid-1950s but these arguments seem to have largely escaped the attentions of tourism scholars. Current tourism research is ambivalent towards, on the one hand, a form of empiricism that proceeds along falsification lines (see Deduction) and, on the other, a reluctance to acknowledge the sociology of scientific knowledge argument (see Constructionism, Critical Theory and Paradigm). These twin 'blind spots' in the tourism academy result in the critique that contemporary orthodox tourism studies is weak, because it is both atheoretical and ahistorical. To these blinkers we should add only scant attention to developments in Realism wherein some of the distances between the positions of rationalism and empiricism are shortened.

Consequentially, we would conclude that the brand of Empiricism in evidence in tourism studies can be characterised as a form of 'weak' or 'naive' empiricism. The result is a tendency to a slow, confirmative and uncritical knowledge accumulation – what Kuhn described as 'normal' science. Franklin and Crang observe that this has resulted in 'Studies (that) have generally been restricted to a vision of tourism as a series of discrete, localised events' (2001: 5) an assertion that is a 'trouble' for tourism studies. It is worth also reading Xiao and Smith's (2006) specific response to Franklin and Crang's claim and to further reflect on the influence of empiricism and rationalism in these authors' subsequent, and divergent, analyses of the growth of tourism knowledge. We would simply note here that such an outcome in tourism knowledge is quite the opposite of the original intention of the founders of Empiricism, to challenge authoritative knowledge.

HISTORICAL DEVELOPMENT

The origins of the philosophy of Empiricism is largely attributed to the 18th-century philosophers Locke, Berkley and Hume. During the rise to prominence of scientific knowledge in the Enlightenment period, Empiricism provided a radical break from the received view that knowledge was based upon ancient texts, religious faith and systematic philosophy. Empiricism involved both a radical critique of claims to knowledge and the methods by which they were justified. In their place it insisted that any criticism of Empiricism be answered in terms of evidence that was open to anyone. Consequentially it opened a challenge to all forms of authority. Its radical beginnings have now been overtaken, however, and in its late 20th century form Empiricism (and its most common expression in the social sciences – logical positivism) hold a somewhat negative connotation of a largely discredited body of thought.

The emergence of Empiricism and its dispute with rationalism was cast by 19th-century historians of philosophy as one of the 'big' debates in Western philosophy. To simplify the two positions Woolhouse writes '(An Empiricist) will hold that experience is the touchstone of truth and meaning and that we cannot know, or even sensibly speak of, things which go beyond our experience. A rationalist ... holds that pure reason can be a source of knowledge and ideas; what we can meaningfully think about can transcend, and is not limited by, what we have been given in experience' (1988: 2) We can see here the origins of the tensions between data and theory that permeate debates in the philosophy of science (see also Critical Realism, Realism, Deduction, Positivism).

DESCRIPTION

Central to classical Empiricism was a conception of the mind as 'tabula rasa' or 'blank tablet'. What could be known about the world is only what the world cares to tell us. It must be observed neutrally and dispassionately through sense data. Only after this can the mind begin to formulate ideas or concepts that would be subject to further rounds of observation.

POTENTIAL CRITICISM

The empiricists denial of an 'outer world', a world beyond individual experience, proved to undermine classical empiricism but provides a continuing source of critique of more extreme and contemporary forms of rationalism.

CROSS REFERENCES

Critical Realism, Deduction, Experiment, Interview/Focus Group, Positivism, Realism, Survey.

FURTHER READING

Generic

Hammersley, M. (2004) Empiricism, in M. Lewis-Beck, R. Bryman and T.F. Liao (eds), *The SAGE Encyclopaedia of Social Science Research Methods*, Vol. 1. Thousand Oaks, CA: Sage. pp. 306–7.
Woolhouse, R.S. (1988) *The Empiricists*. Oxford: Oxford University Press.

Tourism specific

Franklin, A. and Crang, M. (2001) The trouble with tourism and travel theory?, *Tourist Studies*, 1: 5–22.
Xiao, H. and Smith, S.L.J. (2006) Case studies in tourism research: a state-of-the-art analysis, *Tourism Management*, 27: 738–49.

key concepts in
tourism research

Epistemology

Definition The theory of knowledge (Greek: episteme).

RELEVANCE

As for the previous key concept – Empiricism, you cannot do research without the key concept of Epistemology. A difference from Empiricism is that while nearly all of your tutors and supervisors would be comfortable being called an empiricist at least at some time in their academic careers, it is less likely that they would embrace the key concept of epistemology. This is because it often goes unacknowledged and is taken for granted as a commonsense set of assumptions that underlie research activity. The question for you to answer is how important is it for your particular research project and we would be the first to admit that this rather depends on the academic level of study. We would assert that in nearly all social science doctoral level research the presumption would be that the student engages with epistemological argument as a part of mounting a defence of their research thesis. For masters students, the matter of relevance of an explicit discussion of Epistemology in a thesis will depend largely on the expectations set by both the academic disciplines in which the topic is set and those of the supervisor. For undergraduates, well it is almost certainly not required but if you want to impress your dissertation markers then making a coherent argument around Epistemology should translate into extra credits. Beware, though, a poorly constructed and incoherent argument might just have the opposite effect.

APPLICATION

To talk about epistemology is to engage with long-standing arguments in the philosophy of the social sciences about ways of knowing the social world. We take the view that knowledge is a social product originating in communities that are governed by norms and concomitant power-relations. Any notions of truth are embedded in these human interactions.

For the most part tourism scholarship has tended to float above these debates rather than engage with them directly. This is not the case for Botterill who set out to make explicit the implicit epistemological ground in the work of five of his doctoral candidates and he argued that finding a satisfactory position on epistemology was central to the legitimacy of knowledge claims in tourism, 'Opening to the epistemological question would invite not just an enrichment of interdisciplinary tourism research but would also carry with it the project of shaping public discourse around tourism, to take on board the ethical and moral dimensions of the much acclaimed world's largest industry' (2001: 212).

More recently Belhassen and Caton have observed that tourism research resembles an 'institutionalised norm-governed site of conversation' (2009: 336) in which a post-foundationalist epistemology constitutes a field of heterogeneous philosophical perspectives. They analyse the tourism field as a linguistic process, always conditioned by power, and develop a framework for exploring knowledge 'progress' that includes: the creation and adjustment of concepts and models, the production and promotion of new interpretations and understandings, and the employment of these interpretations for problem solving linked to the needs of practitioners and policymakers. Theirs is a view of tourism epistemology that is inspired by a cultural approach to the study of academia in which disciplines are seen as tribes who maintain themselves as segregated academic clans. A problem that arises from this image of academia is captured in the question of what criteria are available to evaluate the superiority of one interpretation over another, without an internal 'standard of scienticity' like Popper's (1963) notion of 'falsifiability' in the empiricist tradition. Consequently, with this question of how we determine the worth of the different accounts of tourism, produced on different epistemological premises, then we arrive at the essence of the philosophy of science.

Tribe (2006: 361) sets the tone by stating that 'despite many truths being established, the whole truth about tourism is left untold, resulting in gaps, silences and misconstructions'. After this observation he adopts a social constructionist approach to study tourism in its cultural situatedness. Based upon Lewin's notion of a force-field, the tourism discourse has been analysed in its knowledge production-activities. In a reaction against the domination of positivism in this field, subjectivity is allowed in a reflexive and perspectivist and even autoethnographic (Botterill, 2003) context, which reveals the interplay of self with research. At the end of his article Botterill appeals to foreground ontology because this is the 'critical realist' answer to the concomitant epistemo-logical problems involved in the subjectivist approach. Similar appeals, but from very different epistemological grounds, are found for post-disciplinarity (Coles et al., 2005), postmodernity (Lyotard, 1984), criti-cal (Franklin and Crang, 2001: 6) and discursive (Foucault, 1971, 1980) perspectives and changing traditions (Jafari, 2003). This has introduced a cacophony of antagonistic voices (Tribe, 2006: 367).

In the face of this assault, Jamal and Hollinshead note that, 'founda-tionalist assumptions of truth, objectivity and validity are being slowly relinquished' (2001: 63) and they consider new criteria from which to judge tourism knowledge but taken from within an interpretive practice 'in the interstices and in-between third spaces of diasporic human exist-ences' (2001: 75) that they argue characterises tourism research in the current network-society. For example, they want to suggest that validity should be recast as 'never a given but is open to the unforeseen coming and goings of the world' (Jardine, 1998: 6). We can see here how, despite the objections to 'internal' criteria of judgement, it is very difficult to escape questions such as validity and in this sense 'many interpretive researchers still cling to the shadows of "valid" and "objective" research, regardless of whether the study is of a quantitative or qualitative ilk' (Jamal and Hollinshead, 2001: 76).

As a contrast and in line with the more 'externalist' tradition of studying scientific knowledge production that emphasises cultural con-text and social practices (that started with Kuhn, 1970), some recent studies (Honggen Xiao and Smith, 2006, 2008; Tribe, 2010; Baggio et al., 2010) have been carried out on the tourism academic community itself. These studies also contribute to our understanding of the disputes in epistemological argument within the tourism academy

HISTORICAL DEVELOPMENT

Reputedly, Isaac Newton was awakened from his dreams under an apple tree as a result of a famous apple falling on his head. Subsequently, he seems to have discovered the laws of gravitation. From this event we can demonstrate the distinction between two concepts: ontology and episte-mology. Since the existence of apple trees, apples have been falling, in most cases directly onto the ground. Although we need to have the use of language to make this statement, very few people tend to deny this as an ontological fact. In contrast, scientists, such as Newton, have since the Enlightenment era sought to formulate theories about this ontological event.

This is precisely what Newton did, he formulated – epistemologically – the laws of gravitation which added something to our understanding of apples falling as a result of gravitational forces in the universe.

Since antiquity another fundamental distinction has been made between knowledge (*episteme*) and opinion (*doxa*). The former is associated with timeless, universal truths and with definite answers to the questions as to why things are the way they are associated with thoughts and related to points of view, typical for an individual, group or period. A serious researcher strives for knowledge and science distinguishes itself by this most respected search for truth. How to reach truth through science has always been an important question in epistemology. Put in more philosophical terms: 'How is it possible that a knowing subject constitutes a truthful image of the world of the object (nature)?'

Popper's answer to that question dominates the current debate, at least in the natural sciences. In his critical rationalism he invokes the rationalism of Descartes arguing that theories (originating in the mind of the subject) precede the gathering of facts (the object). First, scientists should propose theories and develop hypotheses prior to the gathering of facts that are then used to attempt to falsify the hypotheses. In the longer term these, or competing hypotheses, are 'corroborated'. The methodology that has been deduced from this principle, guarantees the distinctive status of scientific knowledge from other types of knowledge, such as religious or everyday commonsense. Through this procedure science approaches a truthful description of the objective world, but without ever being sure of its truth.

As we have discussed elsewhere in this book (see Deduction), in social science this image of science is not self-evident at all. Kuhn (1970) introduced an alternative argument based around the idea of a Paradigm. Here, the progress of knowledge is not guaranteed by 'internal' scientific criteria but, in short periods of scientific revolutions, scientists move from one set of basic assumptions about the world, theories and methodologies (a paradigm) to another set. This process looks more like a conversion to another belief, or should be more understood by a sociological or psychological group-analysis, and is perhaps easier to accept in the social sciences than the scientific criterion like falsification. Kuhn's notion of a Paradigm seems to be more apposite to the way in which the social sciences operate.

For Foucault (1980) a change of the dominant episteme, such as that described by Kuhn as a period of abnormal science, takes place in a much broader sense and is anchored in an historical period of society as a whole and not just in a branch of science. In his treatise on the sociology of knowledge Foucault explores the relationship between class, or other group formations, and the (biased) type of knowledge that has been developed from their position in society. In particular he argued that in the 20th century, the idea that knowledge could exist independently of powerful interests in society lost its integrity completely. What was produced as knowledge was only an affirmation of itself.

As a counterpoint, Mannheim (1997) developed his free floating intelligentsia (*freischwebende Intelligenz*) as the key position of the intellectual who would produce knowledge from as distant and as objective a position as possible. Mannheim wanted to defend the power of the intellectual to remain in some sense extracted from society. The tensions between these two positions are very evident in many university settings today, as our section on Evaluation Research in this book demonstrates.

More fundamentally these different views of the production of knowledge, here expressed as differences in the arguments of Foucault and Mannheim, once again, re-opens the question about the difference between natural and social sciences, a highly relevant epistemological topic with a long history. Social science is sometimes characterised as being at the crossroads of the natural sciences and the humanities (see the writings of Schleiermacher, Dilthey, Weber and Gadamer). Thus far we have emphasised a scientific answer to the epistemological question, however, in the humanities, especially since the 19th century, another way of thinking dominates. Crucial in this is the concept of interpretations of meaning (doxa's) and the privileging of interpretation-techniques (see Hermeneutics) to promote understanding of reality rather than the explanation of reality through causality found in science.

Interpretations are located within research perspectives and the approach it promotes results in a proliferation of interpretations with as a main epistemological question: 'what is an acceptable interpretation?'. In response to this we have two quite different arguments. On the one hand, Ricoeur (1983) provides an optimistic response. He argues that despite the plethora of interpretations it is possible, over a historical era, to find coherence. Derrida (2007), on the other hand, rejects any possibility of coherence, delighting in difference, not similarity. Interpretations come from 'everywhere', are all subject to deconstruction and are thus meaningless and not meaningful. Critiques of knowledge production such as these have had a significant influence over the cacophony of voices within the social sciences and, where they are heard, within tourism knowledge production as well. The epistemological debate within the social sciences has moved a long way from the original positivist idea of a 'uniform science'.

CROSS REFERENCES

Hermeneutics, Paradigm, Positivism.

FURTHER READING

Generic

Derrida, J. (2007) *Jacques Derrida: Basic Writings*. London: Routledge.

Foucault, M. (1971) *L'ordre du discours*. Paris: Gallimard.

Foucault, M. (1980) *Power/Knowledge: Selected Interviews and Other Writings 1972–77*. Brighton: Harvester Press.

Gadamer, H. (1975) *Truth and Method*. New York: Continuum.

Kuhn, T. (1970) *The Structure of Scientific Revolutions*. Chicago, IL: University of Chicago Press.

Lyotard, J. (1984) *The Postmodern Condition: A Report on Knowledge*. Manchester: Manchester University Press.

Mannheim, K. (1997) *Collected Works of Karl Mannheim*. London: Routledge.

Popper, K. (1963) *Conjectures and Refutations: the Growth of Scientific Knowledge*. London: Routledge and Kegan Paul.

Ricoeur, P. (1983) *Hermeneutics and the Human Sciences*. Cambridge: Cambridge University Press.

Tourism specific

Baggio, R., Scott, N. and Cooper, C. (2010) Network science: a review focused on tourism, *Annals of Tourism Research*, 37 (3): 802–27.

Belhassen, Y. and Caton, K. (2009) Advancing understandings: a linguistic approach to tourism epistemology, *Annals of Tourism Research*, 36 (2): 335–52.

Botterill, D. (2001) The epistemology of a set of tourism studies, *Leisure Studies*, 20: 199–214.

Botterill, D. (2003) An autoethnographic narrative on tourism research epistemologies, *Loisier et Société*, 26 (1): 97–110.

Botterill, D., Haven, C. and Gale, T. (2003) A survey of doctoral theses accepted by universities in the UK and Ireland for studies related to tourism 1990–1999, *Tourist Studies*, 3 (1): 283–311.

Coles, T., Hall, C.M. and Duval, D.T. (2005) Mobilising tourism: a post-disciplinary critique, *Tourism Recreation Research*, 30 (2): 31–42.

Franklin, A. and Crang, M. (2001) The trouble with tourism and travel theory, *Tourist Studies*, 1 (1): 5–22.

Honggen, X. and Smith, S. (2006) The making of tourism research: insights from a social sciences journal, *Annals of Tourism Research*, 33 (2): 490–507.

Honggen, X. and Smith, S. (2008) Knowledge impact: an appraisal of tourism scholarship, *Annals of Tourism Research*, 35 (1): 62–83.

Jafari, J. (2003) Research and scholarship: the basis of tourism education, *Journal of Tourism Studies*, 3 (1): 6–16.

Jamal, T. and Hollinshead, K. (2001) Tourism and the forbidden zone: the underserved power of qualitative inquiry, *Tourism Management*, 22 (1): 63–82.

Jardine, D.W. (1998) Learning to love the invalid. Manuscript in process, Faculty of Education, University of Calgary.

Tribe, J. (2006) The truth about tourism, *Annals of Tourism Research*, 33 (2): 360–81.

Tribe, J. (2010) Tribes, territories and networks in the tourism academy, *Annals of Tourism Research*, 37 (1): 7–33.

Ethical Practice

Definition A moral stance that seeks to promote high professional standards in social research and to protect both respondents and researcher from harm.

RELEVANCE

This one is a 'no-brainer', not just relevant but an essential key concept to all tourism research projects at any level.

APPLICATION

Given the definition above, why do we include ethical practice as a key concept in tourism research? Is it likely that tourism research is immoral? What evidence is there that ethical practice is not what it should be in tourism research? What evidence is there that the tourism research community needs to be held accountable for its ethical practices?

Answers to these questions might be found in published accounts of ethical practices in tourism research. On this occasion the literature is not particularly helpful. With the few exceptions of Hartman (1988) who refers to the ethical dilemmas of participant observation, Jennings (2001) who provides a chapter in his textbook guide to carrying out tourism research, and Andriotis (2010) who discusses the ethics of covert non-participant observation on a public nude beach, explicit references to ethical practices in tourism research are difficult to find. We might conclude from published accounts, therefore, that ethical practice is something of a 'black box' for the tourism research community. An exception is Moscardo's (2010) recent chapter on tourism research ethics and readers are encouraged to supplement their study of this key concept by reading her chapter.

Perhaps the paucity of public discussion of ethical practice in tourism research is counterbalanced by a great deal of private discussion among tourism researchers. For example, at the Critical Tourism Studies conference in Zadar in 2009 an attempt to mobilise around ethical practice in tourism research generated considerable interest among delegates but this has yet to have generated a public document (for a comparator example from leisure studies see Fleming and Jordan [2006]). Similar discussions are scheduled for the Tourism Education Futures Initiative Summit 2011 'Activating Change in Tourism Education' in Philadelphia in May 2011. McCabe and Stokoe (2010) also provide a pointer to where private discussions might be held when they inform readers that their study of 'holiday talk' had received 'ethical approval of a UK university'.

Formal ethical scrutiny, and the private discussions that surround it, has been on the rise in many of the anglophile institutions in which tourism research is generated, but there is no systematic evidence of the extent of ethical scrutiny across the national systems of social knowledge production in tourism. From our personal knowledge there are very distinct differences, for example, between universities in the UK and the Netherlands in the practices of ethical scrutiny even within a single Western European tradition in the social sciences. Given this example, the potential for differences between say Confuscian and Western interpretations of ethical practice in the social sciences is at least a question that deserves greater attention in the tourism academy.

There are no internationally agreed ethical codes of practice in social research, nor might there ever be, given that a universal ethical code would only be possible from a universal moral order (Iphofen, 2009).

It is surprising, therefore, that given the volume and extent of tourism research across the globe little specific space has yet been found within the tourism research academy to publicly reflect on the state of ethical practices in tourism research.

HISTORICAL DEVELOPMENT

The contemporary concern for ethical behaviour in research stems from the evidence presented at the trials of prominent Nazi leaders for crimes against humanity. The activity of Nazi medical scientists who conducted inhumane medical trials on concentration camp prisoners, among other groups, in the name of scientific progress, was roundly condemned. The Nuremberg code of 1947 sought to ensure that the abuse of power demonstrated by scientists under National Socialism in Germany and its occupied territories and the harm caused to the subjects in experiments, should never be repeated.

These events had a profound influence on ethical practices in scientific research and have developed into comprehensive processes of ethical scrutiny. In the social sciences the effects of research interventions are clearly not of the same potential magnitude for harm but the fundamental principle of maintaining trust between the research professionals and society is equally paramount. Handling the competing principles of being a good researcher and asking penetrating questions has to be balanced with not interfering unduly in peoples' lives. The argument here is that the best way to achieve this is to attend to, and be seen to attend to, ethical practice.

Abuses of power in research involving threats, bribery, coercion, corruption and thinly veiled justifications of deception are all possible when research involves human subjects. Honesty underpins the whole enterprise of knowledge production and the invention of data, lying about the success of methods, suppressing findings and the selective reporting of data that support a position all threaten the collapse of knowledge production. Judgements of what is morally right and what is expedient is often experienced intensely and uncomfortably by researchers.

DESCRIPTION

Ethical practices are formulated on a rigorous array of interrogations about:

ethical practice

- the necessity and justification of the research;
- the potential risks of harm to individuals/groups/society;
- the potential benefits to individuals/groups/society;
- respondent selection and the management of informed consent;
- the ongoing monitoring of safety of participants and researchers;
- strategies adopted to maintain privacy and confidentiality;
- the vulnerability of the respondents;
- the dissemination of the findings;
- the archival/destruction of data at the close of the project

Iphofen (2009) provides a useful 'Ethical Review Checklist' and a comprehensive discussion of ethical decision making in his recent monograph.

Ethical practice during the conduct of investigations is premised on three platforms; informed consent, the protection of respondent identity, and that no harm is done to respondents. Informed consent implies that the respondent understands what the research is about, who is undertaking and financing it, why it is being undertaken and how it will be disseminated. This should be communicated in terms that are meaningful to the respondents. Under informed consent protocols, respondents should also be advised that they can terminate their involvement for any reason.

Informed consent presents challenges for tourism researchers who adopt forms of social research that use observation and covert methods. If a researcher is attempting to make observations in the field and to minimise the likely 'effect' they might have on the situation under observation, then obtaining informed consent prior to the observation is undesirable. In some cases, post hoc informed consent is a possible strategy wherein respondents are informed of the research after the event but in many field settings this is simply not practical.

Research into organisations, where the researcher is inside or joins a particular organisation for the purposes of the research also presents challenges as the questions of 'when does the research start and stop?' and 'who therefore is a respondent in the research?' are difficult to define. Many Action Research projects place the researcher in this position on the matter of informed consent. Even the assumed benign 'mystery shopper' is problematic under informed consent, where organisations are not pre-warned of their presence, yet it is regularly practiced by tourism researchers at all levels from undergraduates upwards.

Issues of anonymity of respondents are handled by well established protocols for the recording and reporting of spoken and written data. The matter of the privacy of respondents takes a particularly tricky twist in Visual Methods where images are part of the data. Can locations be disguised and identities be protected in visual data without changing the interpretation and meaning of the image? At what point is an image an unacceptable intrusion of privacy? These questions are heard in normative discussions in respect of the many visual surveillance techniques now commonly used to 'police' both public and private spaces but for tourism social researchers they pose particularly tricky dilemmas of ethical practice. We agree with Moscardo when she says that:

> While it is not clear that a code of research ethics specific to tourism is necessary, debate about such a code could be useful in stimulating awareness of this issue. It might also be useful to begin such a process by recognising that the issue exists in tourism, encouraging critical reflexivity on the part of researchers, support deliberate and careful analysis of research contexts and conduct debates about the roles and responsibilities of researchers. These actions could be embedded in tourism education, recognised at tourism research meetings and tackled by existing tourism research associations. (2010: 213)

POTENTIAL CRITICISM

Objections to ethical practices in social research arise not from the principles they seek to promote but are limited to the institutionalising tendencies in ethical scrutiny. For some social scientists these amount to a de-professionalising of the social sciences and an obstructive and inhibiting barrier to the free conduct of social science research.

CROSS REFERENCES

Action Research, Ethnomethodology, Visual Methods.

FURTHER READING

Generic

Iphofen, R. (2009) *Ethical Decision-Making in Social Research: A Practical Guide.* Basingstoke: Palgrave Macmillan.

ethical practice

Tourism specific

Andriotis, K. (2010) Heterotopic erotic oases: the public nude beach experience, *Annals of Tourism Research*, 37 (4): 1076–96.

Fleming, S. and Jordan, F. (2006) *Ethical Issues in Leisure Research*. Eastbourne: Leisure Studies Association.

Hartman, R. (1988) Combing field methods in tourism research, *Annals of Tourism Research*, 15 (1): 88–105.

Jennings, G. (2001) *Tourism Research*. Chichester: Wiley.

McCabe, S. and Stokoe, E. (2010) Have you been away? Holiday talk in everyday interaction, *Annals of Tourism Research*, 37 (4): 1117–40.

Moscardo, G. (2010) Tourism research ethics: current considerations and future options, in D. Pearce and R. Butler (eds) *Tourism Research: A 20–20 Vision*. Oxford: Goodfellow Publishers. pp. 203–14.

Ethnomethodology

> **Definition** Researcher participation in people's daily lives, often for extended periods of time, to study the social world as encountered in everyday experience.

RELEVANCE

If you've got lots of time to do your research and have a way of being 'inside' your research topic, then working with Ethnomethodology should prove to be very rewarding. Unless you are funded to undertake fieldwork as a part of your research project then, as is the case with the Key Concepts of Action Research and Grounded Theory, you'll need to be resourceful in making the most of your situation and interests, in order to find ways to incorporate your research activity into already existing social situations. This is because Ethnomethodology requires you to 'live' your research in the sense of getting an insider perspective on your chosen research topic. Immersion in a community or special interest group or even a workplace or tourism adventure always brings with it the challenge of subject/object relations. How can you remain objective about the thing you are studying if, by the participatory nature of Ethnomethodology, you are required to be sensitive to multi-readings of the situations that you immerse yourself in? Consequentially, there are particularly challenging ethical dilemmas in Ethnomethodology; they are not insurmountable but demand constant attention. How will you write about what you find? Do you take the position of the external authority or attempt to sit behind the subjective accounts of those that you study? Fortunately, there are very good guides to doing Ethnomethodology that provide some, but not all, ways out of these dilemmas.

APPLICATION

The contribution of sociology and anthropology in the early formation of tourism studies signals a significant relationship between Ethnomethodology and the development of knowledge in the subject (Nash and Perdue, 2009). This can be explained, in part, by the motive to explore 'other' cultures that is shared by anthropologists and some tourists, thus there is a natural connection between their activities (Galani-Moutafi, 2000). Anthropologists have seen this common trait as both problematic and helpful in their research. McDonald (1987) suggests that researching the tourist renders much contemporary ethnography possible as tourists' expectations of places increases the visibility of their character. More recent ethnographies, however, have demonstrated that interactions between tourists and hosts results in revisions of stereotypical ethnicity (Stronza, 2008) and the creation of a new, tourism, rhetoric of local traditions (Salazar, 2006).

There are a number of useful accounts of the application of Ethnographic methods to the study of tourism (see for example Palmer, 2001; Nash, 2000). A recent special issue of Tourist Studies provides six examples of the application of Ethnomethodology (Frohlick and Harrison, 2008). The method has been applied to some favoured topics including community tourism development (Cole, 2008; Cordoba Azcarate and Duffy, 2006), backpacking (Westerhausen and Westerhausen, 2002), and sex tourism (Frohlick, 2008). A number of significant themes, in addition to the matter of the processes that shape the authenticity of the 'other', have emerged. These include; the influences of the process of globalisation upon the 'local' (Mordue, 2009; Salazar and Moscardo, 2007), the complex patterns of migration and tourism visitation (O'Reilly, 2003; Duval, 2004), and the formation of tourism identities (Pritchard and Morgan, 2005; Palmer, 2005).

Visual ethnography in tourism research has utilised film (Nicholson et al., 2006; Rakic and Chambers, 2009), television (Mordue, 2009) and post-cards (Pritchard and Morgan, 2005). Ethnomethodology has also been used in combination with historical methods (see for example Schmid, 2008) and discourse analysis (Salazaar and Moscardo, 2007). McCabe and Stokoe (2004) have promoted the value of conversational analysis in their work on 'tourism talk' and Janta et al. (2009) demonstrate the application of Ethnomethodology using the internet, in what they call 'netography'.

HISTORICAL DEVELOPMENT

The foundations of Ethnomethodology are understood to have emerged around the middle of the 20th century as a result of the convergence of two sets of ideas – Parsons' Functional Social Theory and Schutz' Phenomenology. Its creation is largely attributed to the work of Harold Garfinkel (Sharrock and Anderson, 1986).

It was in the vanguard of radical reactions to sociology in the 1960s and, for a short time, it was positioned as the basis for a devasting critique of sociological thought. It was also cast as the backcloth to radical social experimentation. This was, in part, inspired by Garfinkel's own teaching methods. Garfinkel had his students do experiments in order to explore sociological ideas. These were 'breach experiments' – attempts to disrupt normative order such as bargaining over the price of goods in shops or to violate the rules of a game or sport. The resulting events were to be observed and reported by the students as ethno-graphic data and commentary upon the establishment of order in social life. Such experimentation was replicated in many sociology classrooms across the USA and Western Europe.

The initial enthusiasm for Ethnomethodology in the radical social movements of the 1960s foundered with the exposure of more and more ethnomethodological output. Rather than providing the much anticipated serious critique of the (Functionalist and Positivist) founda-tions of sociological knowledge the ethnomethodologists insisted upon attention being given to the fragments of data they collected. Consequentially they appeared more and more to be empiricists and not concerned with philosophical and theoretical substance. Findings were deemed trivial and uninteresting. Ethnomethodology suffered a rather spectacular fall from grace in sociology, in circumstances that continue to cast a shadow over its legitimacy in the social sciences.

The preoccupation with the world as it appears to 'common sense' derives from the philosophical position of phenomenology. Garfinkel's insistence that sociology should begin with the world of commonplace experience, in order to comprehend a pre-theorised functionality of the social world, led to the generation of micro-studies best elucidated in the development of conversational analysis (for an explanation within tourism studies see McCabe, 2007). It has also led to accusations that it is preoccupied with subjective phenomena (see also the Kantian noumena/phenomena distinction in Constructionism). But as Sharrock and Anderson (1986:10) insist, "The aim [of Ethnomethodology] is not to displace objectivity with subjective experience but to discover how objectivity can originate in experience". This is succinctly demonstrated by Stampe's (2008) study of the complex reality of daily life in tourist settings in Upper Midwestern USA.

DESCRIPTION

Ethnography rests on the methods of participant observation and interviewing. The researcher commits to 'engagement with' and 'participation in' everyday situations of social life. The ethnographic way of knowing builds upon inter-subjectivities and interactions to produce an exchange of perspectives between the researcher and the 'Other' (Atkinson, 1995).

The emphasis on the 'ethnographic present' calls for an alternative to the linear, and orthodox, 'read then do then write' model of social research and Crang and Cook (2007) suggest that doing ethnography requires a much looser interaction of these three core research activities. In this they emphasise the inevitable intersubjectivity of ethnography and call for attention to omnipresent power/knowledge relations in research. Consequentially, any claim by the researcher to have isolated 'other' cultures from broader global shifts in political and economic processes or to isolate presents and pasts or individuals from societies in which they live (and research) must recognise a contingent and subjective boundary to knowledge production. Thus, ethnographic accounts produce partial and positioned knowledge within a web of interdependencies. The inevitable relativism suggested by this viewpoint can be counteracted by attention to what Crang and Cook (2007) describe as "rigorous subjectivity" (p,15)

They suggest three aspects to rigorous subjectivity. First, theoretical sampling as a substitute for population sampling: The researcher negotiates to gain selective access to appropriate groups of people who are living through the research problem and who can teach the researcher about the topic under enquiry from a number of perspectives. Second,

ethnomethodology

83

the recognition of theoretical saturation: Here the researcher acknowledges that there are only so many discourses that surround a research topic within a particular interest community and when these begin to be repeated then theoretical saturation has taken place. It is time to move on to another interest group or into an analysis phase. Third, the development of theoretical analysis: In order to have confidence in her/his own study the researcher must engage with other researcher accounts of the phenomenon. In this way the differences between research accounts, and their commonalities, help to shape the context in which the researcher makes their own judgements.

POTENTIAL CRITICISM

Contrary to the emphasis on collaboration between the researcher and the researched in the research process, the tradition in Ethnographic writing is to privilege the researcher voice. The author/researcher somehow becomes detached from his/her immersion in the field. This 'realist' practice has come under attack from several directions, but most notably from feminist and postmodernist perspectives, and there have been many attempts at producing a 'dialogic' ethnography that represents the research in different voices and through textual experimentation.

The examples of the application of Ethnomethodology in tourism studies provided above also tangle with this critique. At the heart of this debate is the apparent contradiction in Ethnomethodology – that engagement between researcher and situation is essential but so also is the privileging of an author-evacuated account in the representation of the research outcomes. In response, researchers have problematised this apparent contradiction (see for example Harrison, 2008) while others continue with the tradition of an authoritative, third-person, researcher voice (see for example Ypeij and Zorn, 2007).

CROSS REFERENCES

Ethical Practice, Interview, Narrative

FURTHER READING

Generic

Atkinson, P.A. (1995) Ethnography: Style and Substance. In I. Maso, P.A. Atkinson, S. Delamont and J.C. Verhoeven (eds) *Openness in Research*, Assen: Van Gorcum pp. 51–63.

Crang, M. and Cook, I. (2007) *Doing Ethnographies*. London: Sage.

Sharrock. W. and Anderson, B. (1986) *The Ethnomethodologists*. Chichester, Sussex: Ellis Horwood.

Tourism specific

Cole, S. (2008) Living in hope: tourism and poverty alleviation in Flores? In P. Burns and M. Novelli (eds), *Tourism Development: Growth, Myths and Inequalities*, CABI, Wallingford, UK (pp. 272–289).

Córdoba Azcárate, M. and Duffy, R. (2006) Between local and global, discourses and practices: rethinking ecotourism development in Celestún (Yucatán, México), *Journal of Ecotourism*, 5, 97–111.

Duval, D. T. (2004) Conceptualising return visits – a transnational perspective. In T. Coles and D.J. Timothy (eds) (2004) *Tourism, Diasporas and Space*, Routledge, London, (pp. 50–61).

Frohlick, S. (2008) Negotiating the public secrecy of sex in a transnational tourist town in Caribbean Costa Rica, *Tourist Studies*, 2008, 8, 19–39.

Frohlick, S. and Harrison, J. (2008) Special Issue: Engaging ethnography in tourist research, *Tourist Studies*, 8, 5–140.

Galani-Moutafi, V. (2000) The self and the Other. Traveller, ethnographer, tourist. *Annals of Tourism Research*, 27, 203–224, 39.

Harrison, J. (2008) Shifting positions, *Tourist Studies*, 8, 41–59.

Janta, H., Ladkin, A., Baum, T., Devine, F. and Hearns, N. (2009) Polish migrant labor in the hospitality workforce: implications for recruitment and retention. *Tourism Culture & Communication*, 9, 5–15.

McDonald, M. (1987) Tourism: chasing culture and tradition in Brittany. In M. Bouquet and M. Winter (eds) *Who from their labours rest? Conflict and Practice in Rural Tourism*, Aldershot, UK: Avebury.

McCabe, S. (2007) The Beauty in the Form: Ethnomethodology and Tourism Studies. In I. Ateljevic, A. Pritchard and N. Morgan (eds) *The Critical Turn in Tourism Studies*. Oxford: Elsevier (pp. 227–244).

McCabe, S. and Stokoe, E. H. (2004) Place and identity in tourists' accounts. *Annals of Tourism Research*, 31, 601–622.

Mordue, T. (2009) Television, tourism, and rural life, *Journal of Travel Research*, 47, 332–345.

Nash, D. (2000) Ethnographic windows on tourism, *Tourism Recreation Research*, 25, 29–35.

Nash, D. and Perdue, R. R. (2009) In the beginning: the making of a book about some beginnings of tourism study, *Tourism Analysis*, 14, 29–36.

Nicholson, H. N., Franklin, A. and Crang, M. (2006) Through the Balkan States: home movies as travel texts and tourism histories in the Mediterranean, c. 1923–39. *Tourist Studies*, 6, 13–36.

O'Reilly, K. (2003) When is a tourist? The articulation of tourism and migration in Spain's Costa del Sol, *Tourist Studies*, 2003, 3, 301–317.

Palmer, C. (2001) Ethnography: a research method in practice, *International Journal of Tourism Research*, 2001, 3, 301–312.

Palmer, C. (2005) An ethnography of Englishness: experiencing identity through tourism, *Annals of Tourism Research*, 32, 7–27.

Pritchard, A. and Morgan N. (2005) Representations of 'ethnographic knowledge': early comic postcards of Wales. In A. Pritchard, N. Morgan and A. Jaworski (eds) *Discourse, Communication and Tourism*. Channel View Publications, Clevedon, UK. pp. 53–75.

Rakic, T. and Chambers, D. (2009) Researcher with a movie camera: visual ethnography in the field, *Current Issues in Tourism*,12, 271–290.

Salazar, N.B. (2006) Touristifying Tanzania: local guides, global discourse, *Annals of Tourism Research*, 33, 833–852.

Salazar, N. B. and Moscardo, G. (2007) Towards a global culture of heritage interpretation? Evidence from Indonesia and Tanzania, *Tourism Recreation Research*, 32, 23–30.

Schmid, K.A. (2008) Doing ethnography of tourist enclaves, *Tourist Studies*, 8, 105–121.

Stampe, J. (2008) Views from here. *Tourist Studies*, 8, 123–140.

Stronza, A. (2008) Beyond the beach: an ethnography of modern travellers in Asia, *Human Organisation*, 67, 244–257.

Westerhausen, K. and Westerhausen, K. (2002) *Beyond the beach: an ethnography of modern travellers in Asia*. Bangkok, Thailand: White Lotus Co. Ltd.

Ypeij, A. and Zorn, E. (2007) Taquile: a Peruvian tourist island struggling for control, *European Review of Latin American and Caribbean Studies*, (no volume/issue) 119–128.

Evaluation Research

> **Definition** Scientific procedures are applied to the collection and analysis of information about the content, structure, and outcomes of programmes, projects and planned interventions. The emphasis is not on creating new knowledge but on improving policy and practice through the application of existing knowledge.

RELEVANCE

You may find yourself being able to double up your research activities by contributing to a funded research programme as a research assistant and taking a specific part of the project for your personal research project. In which case you would do well to consider the key concept we have labelled Evaluation Research. Research conducted as a part of evaluation projects emphasises the contribution that the outcomes have for informing future practice, so being involved in them is a plus for your CV and helpful when looking for a graduate job. However, you should be aware that scepticism about the knowledge created under Evaluation Research can threaten the value of the study's findings for academic audiences.

APPLICATION

The 'bundle' of economic activities that constitutes tourism is replete with examples of 'market failure'. As a consequence, a plethora of correcting interventions have been proposed and implemented by government and the not-for-profit sector. Unsurprisingly then, the tourism research literature is full of studies examining programmes, policies and projects that seek to improve the production of tourism in some way or another. For example, in an article on joint ventures and indigenous tourism enterprises Simonsen (2006) uses Case Studies of two large-scale indigenous tourism enterprises and their divergent responses to insolvency to evaluate directions in indigenous tourism development policy. The article argues that

> the efficacy of collaborative arrangements in large-scale enterprises is limited by the presence of contrasting cultural values, social practices, and economic circumstances, and recommends a greater emphasis on cross-cultural understanding and co-management in the development and management of indigenous tourism enterprises. Acknowledging that small-scale ecotourism and cultural tourism ventures may be more appropriate, the article suggests that even these may not provide the expected benefits and calls for greater caution in indigenous tourism development strategies. (Simonsen, 2006: 107)

In common with the Simonsen example, the mainly academic authors of many evaluation studies have not positioned themselves explicitly within the domain of Evaluation Research, instead they tend to use key words such as 'policy research' or 'stakeholder analysis'. Is this simply a matter of nomenclature or has it disadvantageous implications for the quality of tourism research?

It is undoubtedly the case that the best of this work is embedded within generic social and economic policy analysis. However, much tourism research of this kind is unsupported by references to either policy analysis (such as urban planning) or the Evaluation Research literatures. The danger is that such research underestimates the social and political context in which the application of social science techniques is used. There is, as Pawson (2006) reminds us, a serious complication in Evaluation Research. He puts this point in question form, 'How does evidence speak to power? [or] What do you get if you cross "research" with "real politik"?' (2006: 1). Consequentially, if tourism scholars do not correctly label their work as Evaluation Research, the contextual limits of research findings may be under reported and the transferability of findings to other contexts too willingly assumed (see Ethical Practice). The explicit and limited horizon of Evaluation Research as a vehicle for applying existing knowledge to improving policy and practice may well make it an unattractive label to put on academic output, particularly when such output is increasingly subject to quality assessment that prioritises the creation of new knowledge over its application (see below in Potential Criticism section).

More recent work in tourism, in common with education, health and other policy arenas, has adopted the use of terms such as 'systematic review' and 'meta-analysis' to describe Evaluation Research output. For example, Weed (2006) replicates the enthusiasm for maximisation and re-use of previous research shown in policy studies, management studies, economics and psychology. The author demonstrates the actual and potential contribution of systematic review, meta-analysis and meta-interpretation to tourism research. Brey et al. (2007) use systematic review in order to formulate an agenda for improving future research in the destination resorts field. Systematic review has also been used extensively in travel medicine to make recommendations on illness prevention, see, for example, Dupont (2008) on travellers' diarrhoea prevention.

Black and Weiler's (2005) study of quality assurance and regulatory mechanisms in the tour guiding industry nicely demonstrates most of the characteristics of Evaluation Research; a systematic review of evidence, an evaluation of mechanisms (interventions) and recommendations for improvement in tourist guide performance.

HISTORICAL DEVELOPMENT

In her classic text on evaluation, Carol Weiss (1998) provides the historical background to Evaluation Research. She locates its beginnings to Europe in the 17th century when social reformers attempted to establish links between the conditions of social life and social problems. Subsequent waves of enthusiasm for social intervention grew with the rise of industrialisation and an increase in social problems but as Weiss points out many significant interventions assumed, rather than tested, their efficacy. There was, apparently, no need to evaluate the outcomes of intervention. This prevailing attitude continued through to the mid-20th century when Evaluation Research as we might recognise it today emerged alongside a raft of social policy initiatives in the 1950s in Europe and 1960s in the USA.

Following the introduction of cost benefit analysis in the USA government department of defence in the 1960s and the increasing budgets of departments of education, social services, criminal justice and employment, it was not long before every department hosted its own evaluation unit. The impetus to embrace evaluation was neatly captured by Donald T. Campbell in his vision of the 'experimenting society'.

In his most recent book another influential author on Evaluation Research, Ray Pawson, reminds us that the value placed on evaluation in successive governments cannot be taken for granted as it is subject to a range of factors. Drawing on Solesbury (as cited in Pawson, 2006: 2) he provides an explanation for what he sees as its current popular standing. First, institutional conditions have spawned what some authors have called a 'pragmatic anti-ideological turn in modern politics' that, in turn, has led to the creation of new partnership organisations whose role is to marshal and evaluate evidence to inform government decision making. Second, there has been a 'retreat from the priesthood' in that clients of government policy – corporations, charities, patients, parents, etc. – are less inclined to take professional views on trust and demand supporting evidence. Third, the growth of knowledge management systems has fuelled the availability of evidence. Information technologies not only enable the collection, storage and retrieval of information but they also provide access to knowledge and consequentially provide a wide constituency of interests with legitimacy to challenge and dispute the value of government intervention.

DESCRIPTION

Evaluation Research now embraces both quantitative and qualitative social research methods. This was not always the case. During the middle of the 20th century it was dominated by quantitative methods, in particular quasi-experimental design (see Campbell and Stanley's [1966] classic text). Early critics of experimental research in social settings pointed out that while it is possible to measure the impact of an intervention in certain circumstances this tells us little about the reasons why change has or has not occurred. Arguments for attention to the social process of evaluation that shape the implementation of interventions were further developed by a number of educational researchers, including Guba and Lincoln (1981), and led to an interpretivist turn in Evaluation Research.

Regardless of the nature of data, and it is now generally accepted that both forms of data can be incorporated into Evaluation Research, evaluation studies tend to be either formative or summative. This enduring distinction is largely attributed to Scriven (cited in Clarke, 1999) where he identified formative studies that sought to provide feedback to those who are trying to improve something and summative studies that determine the effectiveness of the intervention on its completion.

Arguments about method have now largely ceased because as Pawson reminds us the signature argument in Evaluation Research is 'What works' (2006: 20). In place of the epistemological (and paradigmatic) argument over method and data sources, Pawson (2006) argues for a more rigorous examination of the ontology of evaluation, again using his preferred style of positing questions such as: 'How do social programmes bring about their effects? How do interventions intervene? What is the nature of causality in the world of policies and programmes?' (2006: 20). He advances a strong realist argument about how change can occur and therefore provides the most theoretically developed approach to undertaking Evaluation Research.

POTENTIAL CRITICISM

The most serious critiques of Evaluation Research draw us back to its essential characteristic – the blending of evidence and political power. The description of Evaluation Research as a 'dark art' is perhaps to overstate the malign possibility but nevertheless it conveys the scepticism displayed by those who hold to the ideal of an independent academy. There is no better place to look for this argument than in the academy itself.

Under the new partnership arrangements, described above, that have driven-up an evidence industry it is the universities themselves who have benefited considerably from the growth in evidence-based government. As Pawson comments 'On a bad day the ivory tower can look awfully like a shopping mall' (2006: 3) as the proliferation of evaluation units, located on the fringes of campuses in spin-out companies or self-funded research organisations, compete for the latest tranche of government or corporate funding. With these developments has come a new market in university leadership recruitment practices wherein senior university staff are appointed to advisory posts within the newly formed government agencies.

In a contra-flow, senior government officials are recruited by universities to head up their evaluation research units. Indeed it is sometimes impossible to keep track of the interchange between 'gamekeeper' and 'poacher' in the world of Evaluation Research. Such 'positioning' games support the accusation that there is a circularity of funding with one arm of government providing funds for another to do Evaluation Research.

The growth in the evidence industry has also enticed the not-for-profit sector into Evaluation Research. Charities who engage in Evaluation Research are also subject to criticism but for a different reason. The proximity of their position as social campaigning organisations with that of evidence providers, is seen as equally problematic to the circulatory arguments described above. For example, in a recent move to secure a stronger financial base, the UK-based organisation Tourism Concern has embarked on a study for a UK government department of the impacts of climate change on sea defences at coastal resorts in England. This work sits somewhat uncomfortably with its high profile campaigning work that is often critical of the UK, and other, governments' positions on matters of social and environmental justice in tourism. The private sector has also emerged as an evidence provider and as Pawson (2006) notes this has led to an increasing use of auditors and regulators to investigate such private bodies and an increase in corporate scandals about the independence of the regulators.

The consequence of all these factors has been to strengthen the arguments of the critics of Evaluation Research who would assert that 'evidence is cynically exploited in the interest of retaining rather than refining the exercise of power' (Pawson, 2006: 4). In view of these criticisms it is our view that it is incumbent on tourism researchers and the publications gatekeepers to be explicit about the particulars of funding and circumstances that have enabled research to be undertaken. If it is Evaluation Research then it should be unambiguously labelled as such if and when it reaches the public domain.

CROSS REFERENCES

Document Analysis, Ethical Practice, Experiment, Realism.

FURTHER READING

Generic

Campbell, D.T. and Stanley, J.C. (1966) *Experimental and Quasi-experimental Designs for Research*. Chicago: Rand McNally, 1966.

Clarke, A. (1999) *Evaluation Research – An Introduction to Principles, Methods and Practice*. London: Sage.

Guba, E.G. and Lincoln, Y.S. (1981) *Effective Evaluation: Improving the Usefulness of Evaluation Results Through Responsive and Naturalistic Approaches*. San Francisco, CA: Jossey-Bass.

Pawson, R. (2006) *Evidence-based Policy – A Realist Perspective*. London: Sage.

Weiss, C. (1998) *Evaluation*, 2nd edn. Upper Saddle River, NJ: Prentice Hall.

Tourism specific

Black, R. and Weiler, B. (2005) Quality assurance and regulatory mechanisms in the tour guiding industry: a systematic review, *Journal of Tourism Studies*, 16 (1): 24–37.

Brey, E.T., Morrison, A.M. and Mills, J.E. (2007) An examination of destination resort research, *Current Issues in Tourism*, 10 (5): 415–42.

Dupont, H.L. (2008) Systematic review: prevention of travellers' diarrhoea, *Alimentary Pharmacology & Therapeutics*, 27 (9): 741–51.

Simonsen, R. (2006) Joint ventures and indigenous tourism enterprises, *Tourism Culture & Communication*, 6 (2): 107–19.

Weed, M. (2006) Undiscovered public knowledge: the potential of research synthesis approaches in tourism research, *Current Issues in Tourism*, 9 (3): 256–68.

·················· Experiment ··················

> **Definition** The most scientifically justified manner to test a causal relationship between the two variables of a hypothesis in a laboratory setting.

RELEVANCE

Helping you to judge the relevance of the Experiment to your research project can be aided by answering some questions? Are you interested in testing the relationship between a small number of variables? Are you able to define and measure the variables with some precision? To what extent can you control for the influence of other variables upon the relationship you wish to measure? How might you design your experiment either within, or to replicate, conditions within a laboratory? Are you competent at handling quantitative data? If you answer these questions in the affirmative then you are well on your way to providing a rare example of the use of the Experiment in tourism research, good luck.

APPLICATION

Within the social sciences, psychology has the closest affinity with experimental research. Consequently, when psychologists turn their attention to tourism it is then that we find the closest examples of the use of the experiment in tourism studies. Psychology's contribution to tourism research has been explained in Pearce and Stringer (1991) as it proceeds by considering psycho-biological and ergonomic studies, cognition, individual difference approaches and the work in social psychology as applied to tourism. In this article selected environmental and cross-cultural studies are also treated as relevant examples of the experimental approach.

Berno and Ward (2005) confirms an 'experimental connection' between the influence of psychology on tourism research. A coherent body of theory, drawn from experimental social and health psychology, synthesised by cross-cultural psychologists for the study of acculturation, has been presented as one foundation of Berno's area of inquiry. An important role for experimental tourism research has also been claimed in an article on tourism motivation and expectation formation (Gnoth, 1997). Reporting on a conference held in 1991 Smith stressed that in future experimental studies, a particular emphasis should be placed on multivariate models of tourist behaviour. This has proved to be the case, particularly in the area of destination choice research (see also Modelling).

Our survey of the tourism literature has failed to find any reported laboratory studies in the tourism literature. This is not to say that the principles of the experiment are absent, but that it would be more precise to characterise their appearance as examples of quasi-experimental or 'natural' experiments (Campbell and Stanley, 1966). Destination choice and image seems to be such a popular topic for the application of quasi-experimental research (Morly, 1994; Lindberg et al. 1999; Andsager and Drzewiecka, 2002; Park and Petrick, 2006; Tasci et al. 2007). For example, in MacKay and Smith (2006) the purpose was to examine age-related differences in memory for tourism advertising, using both text and visual format. With the intervening variables of education and destination familiarity statistically controlled, no memory age-differences were found. Follow-up analyses revealed that advertising format is a determinant of elaborative memory, while age is not.

Prentice and Andersen (2000) explored the relationship between push and pull factors of destination choice. This was accomplished in order to construct a conceptual model, through experimental studies, that explains the conditions under which marketing tools are successful in pleasing the target group for specific destinations. In Frias et al. (2008) the influence of tourists' use of information from internet or travel agencies on the pre-visit destination image has been measured. A quasi-experimental design has been used that offers the advantage of external validity (see below), thus allowing the manipulations of variables in natural environments. The same type of research has been used in Tasci et al. (2007) in order to measure negative biases in the images of tourism destinations brands. Additionally Madrigal (1993) measured differences in perceptions between cities, where perceptions of residents from two Arizonan cities, at different levels of tourism development, were compared in respect of the residents' perceptions of tourism.

Discrete choice experiments (DCAs) have been used (Crouch et al., 2008) in order to examine potential consumer reactions to various options emerging in the embryonic space tourism industry. A DCA is a designed 'choice' experiment in which the variables of interest are systematically varied using statistical design theory. Data from simulated choice experiment avoids selection bias and allows the study of choice alternatives beyond those observed. Also in Velthuijsen and Verhagen (1994) an experimental destination choice analysis has been designed. Another choice modelling approach has been introduced in Lindberg et al. (1999) on the topic of the tradeoffs that residents in host communities are willing to make with respect to tourism's impacts. In another example of choice modelling, an evaluation of tourists' preferences for rural houses is conducted by Royo-Vela (2009) through a stated preference experiment in the northwest area of the Region of Murcia. Finally, in this set of examples, Lee and Crompton (1992) search for novelty in the context of tourism in order to conceptualise its role in the destination choice process and to develop an experimental instrument to measure novelty.

HISTORICAL DEVELOPMENT

In its ideal form an *experimentum crucis* would be a decisive test between two competing theories or hypotheses. In this sense Popper (1959) tried to design such a (thought) experiment in order to decide between

Heisenberg's conception and a consistently statistical interpretation of quantum theory. However, Popper distinguished between a logical and a more sophisticated, methodological way of looking at natural science. In the logical form, a crucial experiment would falsify one of the competing theories. In scientific practice ad hoc hypotheses, auxiliary hypotheses and other instruments help a theory survive at least for a longer period. Nevertheless, in order to test a theory a laboratory experiment counts as the best possible method.

Certainly in the social sciences such decisive experiments, in which one theory succeeds and the other fails, never takes place. When experimenting, social scientists do not speak about the causality of a clear cause and effect, whereas, they do speak about the relationship between two variables, an independent and a dependent variable. A variable is a measurable characteristic of the phenomenon under investigation. An independent variable is the causing variable and the dependent variable is the effect. Causality in social sciences between these two variables has been broken up into three constituent elements: (1) there is a relationship, a (statistical) connection between the two variables; (2) the direction of the relationship between the two variables is clear, for example, age is the (causing) independent variable and frequency of holiday taking is the dependent variable; (3) there are no external influences determining the relationship (the *ceteris paribus* clause). The laboratory experiment is claimed to offer the best condition for testing these three components of causal explanation. The third element is particularly important as it deals with internal validity – that is when the researcher can attribute changes in the experimental group to (only) the treatment effects. The closed condition of the laboratory enables the optimum conditions for the control of intervening variables that might lessen the internal validity of the experiment. One way in which internal validity is improved is through the careful selection and distribution of subjects across the treatment and control groups.

An objection to this type of laboratory research is that the more selection criteria are used in forming the selection of subjects to ensure internal validity, the more the tested situation differs from the natural situation in everyday life. This is known as the problem of external validity. Given the social scientists' realm of inquiry this is why a natural experiment or quasi-experiment is often used outside the laboratory setting in order to increase the external validity. The famous Hawthorne experiments at the Western Electric Company (1924–1932) illustrated this point very well. The original investigation was concerned with the effects of the intensity of lighting upon the workers' productivity. When productivity also improved in the control group, something else could be seen to be the cause, which often happens in natural experiments. The awareness of these other causes started a series of additional experiments that contributed to a new way of management thinking. The pattern of reasoning became clear. The more natural the experiment is in the context of everyday life, the more the external validity rises but often with concessions to internal validity.

DESCRIPTION

Experiments can take many forms or designs. In its simplest form there is an experiment group that receives a stimulus of 'treatment' and a control group. In the experiment group a stimulus will be implemented that is hypothesised to cause a change in the relationship between the two variables to be measured, whereas in the control group there is no such stimulus. At two times ($\times 1$ and $\times 2$) the relationship between the variables will be measured in the two groups, before and after the introduction of the stimulus. In the control group it is expected that there will be no difference between the measurements, whereas in the experimental group there will be a difference between measurement 2 and measurement 1, due to the effect of the stimulus.

POTENTIAL CRITICISM

There are two points of departure in considering a critique of the Experiment. First, there is what we might call an external critique that repeats itself through the writing of this book. Here we mean the general disputes in the philosophy of the social sciences that can be found in the sections on Deduction, Empiricism, Positivism and Constructionism that would countenance or dissent from the value of experiments in social research, as a consequence of their ontological and epistemological assumptions. Second, given the long history of the Experiment, it is not surprising to find an exhaustive literature critiquing its use. Many of these arguments relate to the twin pillars of ensuring reliability and validity in quasi-experimental research.

There are several avenues of critique around validity. Concept validity is an interesting topic for tourism research, because it illustrates differences of opinion between disciplinary perspectives in the social sciences (see also discussion in Epistemology). This can be demonstrated through the case of 'intelligence'. When psychologists measure intelligence they do so by operationalising the concept so that it can be measured via IQ-tests. For some social psychologists and sociologists this would be an overly simplistic measure of intelligence. The concept of intelligence, then, has a more complex nature than the measurement of IQ. Therefore, it might be argued that the researcher is not measuring what she or he wanted to measure. A positivist would solve this validity problem by stating that intelligence is what has been measured in IQ-tests, whereas others would say that intelligence contains certainly more than what has been measured. Validity problems are crucial in the models of explanation in social sciences. There are as many different opinions about the strengths and weaknesses of this positivist way of dealing with validity as there are traditions of thought in social sciences and for some researchers the problem of validity is, simply, unsolvable.

CROSS REFERENCES

Deduction, Empiricism, Evaluation Research.

FURTHER READING

Generic

Campbell, D.T. and Stanley, J.C. (1966) *Experimental and Quasi-experimental Designs for Research*. Chicago, IL: Rand McNally.
Popper, K. (1959) *The Logic of Scientific Discovery*. New York: Harper Row Publishers.

Tourism specific

Andsager, J. and Drzewiecka, J.A. (2002) Desirability of differences in destinations, *Annals of Tourism Research*, 29 (2): 401–42.
Berno, T. and Ward, C. (2005) Innocence abroad: a pocket guide to psychological research on tourism, *American Psychologist*, 60 (6): 593–600.
Crouch, G.I., Devinney, T.M., Louviere, J.J. and Islam, T. (2008) Modelling consumer choice behaviour in space tourism, *Tourism Management*, 30 (3): 441–54.
Frias, D., Rodriguez, M. and Castaneda, J. (2008) Internet vs. travel agencies on pre-visit destination image formation: an information processing view, *Tourism Management*, 29 (1): 163–79.
Gnoth, J. (1997) Tourism motivation and expectation formation, *Annals of Tourism Research*, 24 (2): 283–304.
Lee, T.-H. and Crompton, J.L. (1992) Measuring novelty seeking in tourism, *Annals of Tourism Research*, 19 (4): 732–51.

experiment

Lindberg, K., Dellaert, B. and Rassing, C. (1999) Resident tradeoffs: a choice modeling approach, *Annals of Tourism Research*, 26 (3): 554–69.

MacKay, K.J. and Smith, M.C. (2006) Destination advertising: age and format effects on memory, *Annals of Tourism Research*, 33 (1): 7–24.

Madrigal, R. (1993) A tale of tourism in two cities, *Annals of Tourism Research*, 20 (2): 336–53.

Morly, C. (1994) Experimental destination choice analysis, *Annals of Tourism Research*, 21 (4): 780–91.

Park, S.Y. and Petrick, J.F. (2006) Destinations' perspectives of branding, *Annals of Tourism Research*, 33 (1): 262–5.

Pearce, P. and Stringer, P. (1991) Psychology and tourism, *Annals of Tourism Research*, 18 (1): 136–54.

Prentice, R. and Andersen, V. (2000) Evoking Ireland: modeling tourism propensity, *Annals of Tourism Research*, 27 (2): 490–516.

Royo-Vela, M. (2009) Rural-cultural excursion conceptualization: a local tourism marketing management model based on tourist destination image measurement, *Tourism Management*, 30 (3): 419–28.

Smith, S. (1991) PATA's 1990 conference, *Annals of Tourism Research*, 18 (2): 333–5.

Tasci, A.D.A., Gartner, W.C. and Cavusgil, S.T. (2007) Measurement of destination brand bias using a quasi-experimental design, *Tourism Management*, 28 (6): 1529–40.

Velthuijsen, J.W. and Verhagen, M. (1994) A simulation model of the Dutch tourism market, *Annals of Tourism Research*, 21 (4): 812–17.

·························· Feminism ··························

> **Definition** A social movement that has inspired social theory and distinctive social research methods that both highlight the oppression of women and promote alternative visions of social life informed by the experiences and insights of women.

RELEVANCE

If you accept the arguments of feminist scholars that much research is gender blind, then there is a lot of catching up to do in tourism research and therefore plenty of scope for feminist studies of tourism. Your gender is probably the most important criteria here and while we would argue that it is possible for men to adopt feminist methodologies and study masculinity, studies of women and tourism need to be undertaken by, and for, women. You will also need supervisors who understand the arguments of feminist scholars and, if possible, have practiced feminist research, and no doubt some would argue that there should be at least one woman (and in the case of men's studies, one man) in a supervisory role.

APPLICATION

Feminist analysis in the tourism literature has been a recent phenomenon. Consequentially, the characteristic of published work is of late-stage feminism informed by cultural studies, post-structuralism, postmodernism and social constructionism. Aitchison (2005) provides a thorough review of the antecedents to more recent feminist scholarship in tourism (and see below for a brief review of the historical development of feminist thought in the social sciences). The absence of feminist scholarship in tourism informed by neo-Marxist and radical feminist theory caused by its late uptake compared, say, to leisure studies and sport studies has left open several potential areas of enquiry untouched (see Browne [2009] as an exception). Explorations of women's experiences of holidays from the perspective of domestic labour relations and children's socialisation into class-based gender holiday roles are but two, among many other, omissions in the literature.

Examples of feminist scholarship in tourism have been collected in an edited book on tourism and gender: embodiment, sensuality and experience (Pritchard et al., 2008) and a special issue of *Tourist Studies* (Morgan et al., 2005) on embodiment, gender and sexuality. Several examples of feminist analysis appear in the edited book of the critical turn conference held in Croatia (Ateljevic et al., 2008). As might be expected, women's experiences of travel dominate empirical accounts in the literature, often accompanied by a dismantling of 'malestream' concepts and theories (Wearing and Wearing, 2001; Myers and Hannam, 2008). Explorations have turned from generic accounts of women's travel (Small, 2003; Jordan and Gibson, 2005) to more specific aspects of women's holiday taking, as in the explorations of fear (Wilson and Little, 2008) and eating out on holiday (Heimtun, 2010).

Discussions of feminist epistemology in tourism research can be found in Swain (2004) in relation to the researcher-researched relationship, in

feminism

Mansfield's (2007) account of 'passionate' scholarship and in Humberstone's (2004) account of standpoint theory.

HISTORICAL DEVELOPMENT

The central preoccupation of feminism has been to argue that sexual otherness is a meaningful distinction of social and moral order. Social scientists and social theorists have responded to accounts of sexual otherness by literary scholars, such as Simone do Beauvoir, Virginia Woolf and Germaine Greer, to establish a distinctive agenda in social research that includes gender studies, social exclusion, the body, issues of meaning and identity, and the ethical dimensions of relations between women and men. From a position of gender difference, feminist scholars have challenged the gender-blind presumption in the creation and dissemination of knowledge. Alongside the prioritising of a feminist agenda in a range of social science disciplines, a coterminous critique of method has evolved into a distinctive feminist debate on method, methodology and epistemology.

Commentaries upon feminism within social theory generally agree that there have been several fruitful exchanges over the past half century. Feminist scholars adopted aspects of Marxism to demonstrate the invisibility of women in capitalist production and emphasised the importance of the household as a site of women's oppression through the ordering of power relations between men and women in biological reproduction, the socialisation of children and the reproduction of male labour power.

Radical feminists in the 1960s and 1970s turned attention away from the oppression of capitalism to focus on patriarchy as the central axiom of explanation. This produced a shift in priority from economic to sexual relations, highlighting how men control women's bodies through the institution of marriage, motherhood and heterosexuality. The practical consequences of a radical viewpoint are not without its substantive criticisms but an enduring legacy of radical feminism was to set the body at the centre of feminist theory. Radical feminists argued that because it is the body that performs within the social world any attempts to control or damage it reduces the agency of women.

Explorations of psychoanalytical writings by feminist scholars in the 1980s, particularly those of Jacques Lacan, turned attention to the developmental influences of language, symbols and culture on a child's identity. Feminists argued that the symbolic order (the Oedipal stage of a child's development) marginalises, misrepresents and ultimately excludes women and they called for a subversion of the masculine 'text' with the writing into culture of women's sensuality and eroticism. The resultant emphasis on the anatomical differences between men and women and claims that sexual identity could be reduced to psychosexual processes, based on the body, resulted in accusation that this simply replaced the absence of women in a masculine culture with a fixed identity that might easily become the subject of a new set of misrepresentations.

The juxtaposition of fixed and fluid sexual identity became a central argument to contemporary shifts in feminist analysis as the influences of social constructionist and deconstructionist thought held sway since the 1990s. Here an exploration of difference and sexual otherness evolved into a metaphysics of fluidity that rejects binary oppositions and celebrates difference, change and instability. These debates engage with the fundamental distinction between sex and gender as a basis of otherness moving towards a position that both are indeed social constructions of a particular time and culture.

DESCRIPTION

The claim that knowledge presented as neutral, objective and value-free was, in fact, only partial and gender-biased has led feminist scholars to promote a vigorous debate about the creation of social knowledge. Initially this took the form of the rejection of commonly used quantitative techniques such as the survey questionnaire in favour of more qualitative approaches that were perceived as less invasive methods of data collection and more able to support interpretative approaches to analysis.

More latterly the favouring of qualitative methods has been under challenge from the position that it is not the method itself but the methodological and epistemological frame in which it is used that provides a proper link with the feminist project. A more eclectic set of methods is now quite commonplace.

The emphasis within feminist methodology has been to ensure that research takes place in a non-exploitative and ethically sound manner (see also Ethical Practice). This has required the researcher to counteract any structural inequalities between the researcher and the participants in the study. Such actions involve developing a good rapport with the respondents and maintaining open and honest communications throughout the project. The adoption of different terminology for the respondent, such as co-researcher, and their involvement in research design has also been favoured. Some of these practices have filtered into mainstream social research.

feminism

Perhaps the most significant development has been the move to reflexivity as a way to address power imbalances in the research process. Drawing upon Ramazangolu (2002), Mary Maynard identifies two dimensions to reflexivity. The first relates to 'the assumptions and ethical judgements that frame the research ... how researchers can account for the knowledge they produce' (2004: 380). The second dimension refers to the situatedness of the researcher, 'the personal biography and position in relation to the subject'. As a result feminist scholarship is sometimes characterised by an extensive reflection by the researcher on these matters.

POTENTIAL CRITICISM

The dependence on reflexivity for a defence of objectivity can result in accounts of research that are dominated by procedural matters and researchers' involvement to the extent that 'the complexity of participants' lives are reduced to the researcher's autobiographical history' (Maynard, 2004: 380).

CROSS REFERENCES

Constructionism, Ethical Practice.

FURTHER READING

Generic

Maynard, M. (2004) Feminist research, in M. Lewis-Beck, R. Bryman and T.F. Liao (eds), *The SAGE Encyclopaedia of Social Science Research Methods*, Vol. 1, Thousand Oaks, CA: Sage. pp. 378–81.
Ramazanoglu, C. with Holland, J. (2002) *Feminist Methodology*. London: Sage.
Shilling, C. and Mellor, P.A. (2001) *The Sociological Ambition*. London: Sage.

Tourism specific

Aitchison, C.C. (2005) Feminist and gender perspectives in tourism studies: the social-cultural nexus of critical and cultural theories, *Tourist Studies*, 5 (3): 207–24.
Ateljevic, I., Pritchard, A. and Morgan, N. (eds) (2008) *The Critical Turn in Tourism Studies: Innovative Research Methodologies*. Oxford: Elsevier.
Browne, K. (2009) Naked and dirty: rethinking (not) attending festivals, *Journal of Tourism and Cultural Change*, 7 (2): 115–32.

key concepts in
tourism research

Heimtun, B. (2010) The holiday meal: eating out alone and mobile emotional geographies, *Leisure Studies*, 29 (2): 175–92.

Humberstone, B. (2004) Standpoint research: multiple versions of reality in tourism theorising and research, in L. Goodson and J. Phillimore (eds), *Qualitative Research in Tourism: Ontologies, Epistemologies and Methodologies*. London: Routledge. pp. 119–36.

Jordan, F. and Gibson, H. (2005) 'We're not stupid … but we'll not stay home either': experiences of solo women travellers, *Tourism Review International*, 9 (2): 195–211.

Mansfield, L. (2007) Involved-detachment: a balance of passion and reason in feminisms and gender-related research in sport, tourism and sports tourism. *Journal of Sport Tourism*, 12 (2): 115–41.

Morgan, N., Ateljevic, I., Pritchard, A. and Harris, C. (2005) Tourism and gender: embodiment, sensuality and experience, *Tourist Studies*, 5 (3): 203–302.

Myers, L. and Hannam, K. (2008) Women as backpacker tourists: a feminist analysis of destination choice and social identities from the UK, in K. Hannam and I. Atelievic (eds), *Backpacker Tourism: Concepts and Profiles*. Clevedon: Channel View. pp. 174–87.

Pritchard, A., Morgan, N., Ateljevic, I. and Harris, C. (2008) *Tourism and Gender: Embodiment, Sensuality and Experience*. Wallingford: CABI.

Small, J. (2003) The voices of older women tourists, *Tourism Recreation Research*, 28 (2): 31–9.

Swain, M.B. (2004) (Dis)embodied experience and power dynamics in tourism research, in L. Goodson and J. Phillimore (eds) *Qualitative Research in Tourism: Ontologies, Epistemologies and Methodologies*. London: Routledge. pp. 102–18.

Wearing, S. and Wearing, B. (2001) Conceptualizing the selves of tourism, *Leisure Studies*, 20 (2): 143–59.

Wilson, E. and Little, D.E. (2008) The solo female travel experience: exploring the 'geography of women's fear', *Current Issues in Tourism*, 11 (2): 167–86.

Figurationalism

Definition A research tradition in which evolving networks of interdependent individuals (figurations) influence changes to codes of behaviour via external control and internalised self-control in a 'civilising process'.

RELEVANCE

Throughout this book we have eluded to the relative paucity of theory development in tourism research. We have included Figurationalism as a key concept, because we feel that it offers a way to address this gap. If you are keen to help with this project then an exploration of an aspect of tourism seen through the Figurationalist lens could set a trend in tourism scholarship and you could find yourself in the vanguard of it. In our view, few other recent social theories would seem to have such relevance to the condition of tourism. Tourism itself is surely a prime example of shifts in figurations, the importance of emotion and identity in tourist experience and the matter of 'correct' behaviour of tourists and hosts could be better theorised by reference to Elias' work, we argue. Elias' observations of the state could also open up a new analytical line on private/public sector relations in tourism. Editions of the 19th- and 20th-century travel guides of Baedeker and Muirhead offer a fascinating historical record of tourism and tourist advice that would seem to offer a comparative resource to the courtesy manuals that were so central in Elias's main thesis. It would obviously help if you had sympathetic supervisors well versed in Eliasian theory and method but with the communications resources now available through the internet perhaps this could be achieved by associating with academic groups outside of your own institution.

APPLICATION

Figurational sociology has had scant attention within tourism studies. Teuns (1992) did attempt to bring the works of Norbert Elias to the attention of tourism scholars in his rejoinder on media use in the third world but, seemingly, with little effect. In perhaps the most significant contribution from a figurationalist perspective, Dunning (1996) provided a critique of Urry's *The Tourist Gaze* in his essay 'On problems of the emotions in sport and leisure'. Indeed it is in leisure and sports studies where we can find the closest fit of Figurationalism to the interests of tourism researchers. Lesjo (2000) adopts Elias' game model perspective to analyse the planning processes that surrounded the Winter Olympics in Lillehammer in 1994 and Harris (2005) provides summaries of examples of an Eliasian inspired analysis of football.

The potential of Figurationalism in tourism studies is considerable. We would argue that tourism is a prime example of shifting figurations and the consequential tensions and emotional impact on individuals. The balances of power in tourism destinations (see Lesjo, above), relations between host and guests, the consequences of post-colonial dependencies for the self-determination of tourism destinations are all potential areas for figurationalist studies. For scholars minded to pursue this work then Maguire's (1988) research note would be an excellent starting point.

HISTORICAL DEVELOPMENT

Figurationalism is a sociological approach developed by Norbert Elias, first and foremost in his book *The Civilising Process*, a monumental study of social change in England, France and Germany across six centuries. Elias was coming to the end of his study in the period leading up to the outbreak of the Second World War. As a result of the growing censorship in Germany under National Socialism it was not published until many years later. After 1945 Elias emigrated, first to France and then to the UK where he gained his first permanent academic position at the University of Leicester in 1954 at the age of 57. His students at Leicester included Eric Dunning and Stephen Mennell who both went on to champion his work (Dunning and Mennell, 2003) and demonstrate the potential of Figurationalism, particularly in studies of sport and food. He later moved to the University of Amsterdam where his work was well received and he built an influential group of latter-day scholars of Figurationalism (see http://www.norberteliasfoundation.nl/).

Elias noted in his studies of social change that in all periods of history people form mutual interdependencies (figurations). Notwithstanding the risk of simplification, we might suggest that a contemporary example might be a virtual group of friends on a social networking site. He also observed that figurations were connected in chains of figurations that varied across historical periods. For example, medieval figurations across Europe were fragmented and the chains of interdependency were short. People worked, grew food, reproduced, created families in similar patterns and networks but these patterns were replicated in isolation. Over time and for many different reasons these chains of interdependency expanded, isolation was reduced and new patterns of power and influence were formed.

In particular, Elias observed how the power of an absolute monarch emerged. As the patterns of figurations grew the old order of power based on the ownership of land began to disintegrate. A new figuration of the 'third estate', a kind of middle class if you like of newly wealthy bankers and business leaders, developed in towns and cities and began to challenge the power base of the landed aristocracy in, for example,

figurationalism

the French court. The French monarch recognised that he could play with the loyalties of both groups and in doing so he expanded his own power base. For Elias, so began the processes of centralisation and decentralisation in Europe that had consequences for the shape of Western civilisation up until today. Chains of interdependencies developed from absolute monarchies to the creation of nation states; the establishment of welfare regimes after the Second World War, and to the global village as a new figuration of contemporary times.

The identification of the influence of new figurations is one side of the figurationalist argument. It describes the socio-genesis of different networks of humans. At the same time Elias argued that figurations have enormous influence over emotions and behaviour – the psycho-genesis of figurations. Within figurations he observed how individual needs and drives became moderated by consideration of the best interests of the group. He produced a catalogue of human behaviours that have changed over time that could be explained by the way interdependencies exert external control over human needs and desires. The proposition here is that as peoples' lives become enmeshed in more and more complex chains of interdependence, they have to take into account the different cultural understandings of acceptable codes of behaviour. Raw emotion and primal behaviours become constrained in the interest of maintaining mutual dependencies. For some figurationalists this process is a move towards greater civilisation.

The question of whether society becomes more civilised or not is something that Elias himself refused to be drawn into. Instead, he preferred to point to the fragility of a civilising process built on the shifting sands of figurations. Elias insisted that figurations cannot be understood from a priori knowledge of group norms and rules akin to a functionalist sociological explanation. Neither were they to be explained by reference to some category derived from social conflict theory, a struggle between genders or races for example. He offered then a distinctive sociology that went beyond old divisions in social theory based on a strong historical base with clear cut terminology and considerable explanatory power. In some areas such as family studies, education and the emergence of the welfare state, Figurationalism has proved inspirational. His position within sociology does seem to be in the ascendant. He is now acknowledged as an authority on the history of emotions, identity, violence, the body and state formation. The attention of tourism scholars to his work is long overdue.

DESCRIPTION

Researchers in the figurationalist tradition have adopted a range of social research techniques including Document Analysis and Ethnomethodology. A particularly informative source for Elias, and later for Mennell, was the so-called 'courtesy books' of the pre-modern era. In his essay an 'Introduction to Sociology' Elias demonstrated his unique scholarship in producing an analysis of figurations that combined quantitative and qualitative methods, a methodological approach that was well in advance of anyone else at the time. From the courtesy books he extracted accounts of behavioural codes, advice on sleeping or eating habits for example, and formed a series of extracts in a chronological order of change. He argued that the shifting positions on etiquette suggested deeper structural change – the curve of development from an uncontrolled life to increasing amounts of control in modern societies. By analysing the discourse of texts in this way he made the slow progress of history visible. As Gadi Algazi observes, 'Elias' methodological experimentation with serial analysis and the representation of historical change through curves, lies at the intersection of quantitative and qualitative approaches, of the fascination with the graphic method and established traditions of textual interpretations' (2008: 452).

POTENTIAL CRITICISM

Arising from Elias' work there is a general controversy about the directions of the civilising process (more or less control, various directions instead of one unilinear direction towards self-control).

CROSS REFERENCES

Document Analysis.

FURTHER READING

Generic

Algazi, G. (2008) Norbert Elias's motion pictures: history, cinema and gestures in the process of civilization, *Studies in History and Philosophy of Science*, 39: 444–58.
Dunning, E. and Mennell, S. (2003) *Norbert Elias Volumes 1–4*. London: Sage.

figurationalism

Dunning, E. (1996) On problems of the emotions in sport and leisure: critical and counter-critical comments on the conventional and figurational sociologies of sport and leisure, *Leisure Studies*, 15: 185–207.

Harris, D. (2005) *Key Concepts in Leisure Studies*. London: Sage.

Lesjo, J.H. (2000) Lillehammer 1994. Planning, figurations and the 'Green' Winter Games, *International Review for the Sociology of Sport*, 35 (3): 282–93.

Maguire, J. (1988) Research note: doing figurational sociology: some preliminary observations on methodological issues and sensitizing concepts, *Leisure Studies*, 7 (2): 187–93.

Teuns, L. (1992) Media use in third world research, *Annals of Tourism Research*, 19 (2): 343–7.

Grounded Theory

Definition Grounded theory is an analytical method for constructing theories from inductive qualitative data. Data collection and analysis inform each other in an iterative process as researchers successively make the emerging ideas more abstract.

RELEVANCE

Here we go again, banging on about the absence of significant theory development in tourism research, but this time proponents of Grounded Theory would propose to fill the void by building theory from empirical observations. This is certainly a possible strategy and there are many topic areas in tourism studies that would benefit from such an exploration. However, there are both practical and intellectual caveats to think about before diving in. On practical grounds an ambition to build theory from an immersion in the field requires considerable investment in time and resources. Rather like our advice on Action Research and Ethnomethodology, establishing access to your fieldwork location is best

key concepts in
tourism research

achieved prior to starting your research project, so if you are already heavily involved in an organisation, or with a group of some kind as a volunteer or paid employee, then you are in a better position to try Grounded Theory. One way around this problem, particularly for undergraduate and even masters students, is to label the research as a preliminary exploration of the application of Grounded Theory. From an intellectual standpoint then there are, as we describe below, reservations about the status of the theoretical claims made under Grounded Theory.

APPLICATION

In tourism studies Grounded Theory has been used in a bewildering array of studies. For example, Papathanassis and Knolle (2010) examine online holiday reviews and Lepp (2006) explores the reasons for a dependency on tourism in Bigodi village (Uganda), in which it is concluded that it appears to be the result of traumatic events in the village's past.

Some applications of Grounded Theory aim to construct models. For example, Hunter-Jones (2005) seeks to explain the holiday needs of cancer patients at different stages of their illness, Kim et al. (2009) construct a model of the consumption of locally sourced food on holidays and Ruiz-Ballesteros (2010) develops a model of social ecological resilience as a theoretical framework for community-based tourism in Agua Blanca, Ecuador.

In other applications typologies are constructed. Decrop and Snelders (2005) formulate six types of vacationers by looking at vacation decision making as an ongoing process with many contextual influences. In Hunter's (2008) study of a typology of 'groomed spaces' photographic representations of tourism destinations are deployed in a mixed methods approach. Grounded Theory has been used in connection with Narrative research as in Nimrod's (2008) exploration of retirees' narratives about tourism and with actor-network theory (see Realism) in a study of innovation in a tourism company in the context of French ski-resorts (Paget et al., 2010).

Grounded Theory is used to explore stakeholders' perceptions in the Daintree area of far north Queensland, Australia, because the author argues that there is little pre-existing theory on the role of stakeholder analysis in facilitating sustainable tourism (Hardy, 2005). The same goes for research on the perspectives of tourism policymakers in the turbulent urban planning environment in the city of Leeds, involving communication and negotiation in a social process between people in the

grounded theory

context of wider social and economic change (Stevenson et al., 2008). An interesting point of consideration in this case has been the increased interest in the network approach (Dredge, 2006) that has arisen from the increased complexity of the planning environment and the proliferation of cross-sector partnerships to develop and deliver policies. The inductive, naturalistic approach of grounded theory seems to be a valuable tool to understanding this complexity.

Where there is no theoretical insight available, grounded theory helps to construct such insight in an emergent manner from inductive qualitative data. However, the result is far removed from any notion of a body of coherent theory and we return to this point in our critique of Grounded Theory below.

HISTORICAL DEVELOPMENT

In its initial stages in the 1960s and 1970s in the USA, Grounded Theory was projected as the only qualitative alternative to quantitative research. Its founders, Glaser and Strauss (1967), had been heavily influenced by Symbolic Interactionism with its organic, naturalistic approach to researching social reality and its view of concepts that are sensitising rather than definitive and thus gain their utility and significance from patterned relationships, rather than quantifiable correlations. Some, more objectivist adherents of grounded theory, assume this reality as an external world, with the scientist as a neutral observer and categories as derived from data. More constructivist thinkers place priority on the studied phenomena over the methods of studying it, with grounded theory strategies as tools and the researcher's role as interpretive involved in creating categories. These different interpretations of Grounded Theory go back to a strong disagreement between the two founders, in which there was a difference in viewpoint in relation to the role of induction, deduction and verification and in the way in which data was coded and theory formatted.

DESCRIPTION

In Grounded Theory, data collection, analysis, and theory stand in a reciprocal relationship to each other. An area of study is the starting point and findings are emergent. The aim of the analysis is the development of theories based on the careful examination of empirical data. There are several useful guides to doing Grounded Theory (see, for example, Charmaz, 2006).

Grounded Theory involves an iterative process between data collection and analysis, facilitated by theoretical sampling. It starts with a subject and the gathering of material that is relevant to that subject. From this material, concepts are developed which describe some important aspects of the material in more general terms. This is done by attributing codes to parts of this material, for example, an interview, a fragment of a text, an observation. Codes can then be compared, adapted, improved or specified. This is called the constant comparison method.

This process carries on until the concepts are saturated, which means that new comparisons are not adding additional changes to the existing codes. An important tool in this process is the written memo, in which ideas, important observations or preliminary conclusions are written down as the concepts emerge. Subsequently, concepts (codes) will be connected and systematised insights will be organised and theory is duly constructed.

According to Corbin and Strauss (2008: 61) in this process three types of coding are to be used:

1 open coding, the process of breaking down, examining, comparing, conceptualising, and categorising data;
2 axial coding, a set of procedures whereby data is put back together in new ways after open coding, by making connections between categories;
3 selective coding, the process of selecting the core category, systematically relating it to other categories, validating those relationships and filling in categories that need further refinement and development.

POTENTIAL CRITICISM

Critical attention will be paid to three main points of Grounded Theory as a research tool. The first is about the status of its theories. Is what is produced really 'theory'? Or, is it no more than an empirical generalisation that does not fit into a thoroughly tested theoretical framework? This critique comes mainly from the side of positivist, epistemological vision inspired by the natural sciences. The second is about the notion of 'ground'. Why is the idea of 'grounding' during data collection important? There seems to be at least a glimpse of 'essentialism' in this endeavour to 'ground'. Such 'fixed' ideas about categories of social reality seem somewhat at odds with the emergent thrust of Grounded Theory. The third main point of criticism is about the claim to use and develop inductive knowledge. According to Thomas and James (2006) it is impossible to free oneself of preconceptions in the collection and analysis of data in the way that the founding fathers, Glaser and Strauss, state is necessary.

In the past, there were qualitative methods, other than Grounded Theory methods, that were often considered not scientific. This was especially so within American academic circles, where qualitative research has often been equated to Grounded Theory. This opinion, of course, is criticised by qualitative researchers using other methodologies. More recently, Grounded Theory has often been used as part of a mixed methodology.

CROSS REFERENCES

Deduction, Epistemology, Ethnomethodology, Symbolic Interactionism.

FURTHER READING

Generic

Corbin, J. and Strauss, A. (2008) *Basics of Qualitative Research: Techniques and Procedures for Developing Grounded Theory*. Newbury Park, CA: Sage.

Charmaz, K. (2006) *Constructing Grounded Theory: A Practical Guide Through Qualitative Analysis*. Thousand Oaks, CA: Sage.

Glaser, B.G. and Strauss, A. (1967) *Discovery of Grounded Theory. Strategies for Qualitative Research*. Mill Valley, CA: Sociology Press.

Thomas, G. and James, D. (2006) Re-inventing grounded theory: some questions about theory, ground and discovery, *British Educational Research Journal*, 32 (6): 767–95.

Tourism specific

Decrop, A. and Snelders, D. (2005) A grounded typology of vacation decision-making, *Tourism Management*, 26 (2): 121–32.

Dredge, D. (2006) Policy networks and the local organization of tourism, *Tourism Management*, 27: 269–80.

Hardy, A. (2005) Using grounded theory to explore stakeholder perceptions of tourism, *Journal of Tourism and Cultural Change*, 3 (2): 108–33.

Hunter, W.C. (2008) A typology of photographic representations for tourism: depictions of groomed spaces, *Tourism Management*, 29 (2): 354–65.

Hunter-Jones, P. (2005) Cancer and tourism, *Annals of Tourism Research*, 32 (1): 70–92.

Kim, Y.G., Eves, A. and Scarles, C. (2009) Building a model of local food consumption on trips and holidays: a grounded theory approach, *International Journal of Hospitality Management*, 28 (3): 423–31.

Lepp, A. (2006) Tourism and dependency: an analysis of Bigodi village, Uganda, *Tourism Management*, 29 (6): 1206–14.

Nimrod, G. (2008) Retirement and tourism: themes in retirees' narratives, *Annals of Tourism Research*, 35 (4): 859–78.

Paget, E., Dimanche, F. and Mounet, J-P. (2010) A tourism innovation case: an Actor-Network Approach, *Annals of Tourism Research*, 37 (3): 828–47.

Papathanassis, A. and Knolle, F. (2010) Exploring the adoption and processing of online holiday reviews: a grounded theory approach, *Tourism Management*, 32: 215–24.

Stevenson, N., Airey, D. and Miller, G. (2008) Tourism policy making: the policymakers' perspectives, *Annals of Tourism Research*, 35 (3): 732–50.

Ruiz-Ballesteros, E. (2010) Social-ecological resilience and community-based tourism: an approach from Agua Blanca, Ecuador, *Tourism Management*, 25 (6): http://www.sciencedirect.com/science/article/pii/S0261517710001056 (accessed on 7 August 2011).

Hermeneutics

Definition The study of interpretation theory and the act of interpreting itself.

RELEVANCE

The popularity of what has been referred to as the 'interpretive turn' in tourism research owes its legacy, in the most part, to the key concept of Hermeneutics. If you are interested in studying the multiple perspectives that seem to constitute tourism experiences, then you would do well to start with reading about Hermeneutics. From such a strong conceptual base, the selection and application of qualitative data collection and analysis methods in your study would prepare you for a likely necessary defence of your work that tends, in the main, to favour discursive outputs and multiple conclusions. One solution to this is to present your findings as a series of separate 'voices' on the topic of your investigation,

hermeneutics

rather than mount any, singular, authoritative conclusions. You need to be aware of where Hermeneutics takes you in the social science knowledge creation debate and investing time in understanding the arguments of Constructionism, Realism, Empiricism and Deduction would be, in our view, a wise move, particularly for students at advanced levels of academic awards.

APPLICATION

Fisher's (2004) study of the heritage of Levuka, the former capital of Fiji, provides an interesting example case of Hermeneutics in tourism research. In his chapter he demonstrates 'how tourists and recent non-indigenous residents impose their heritage values on the host community, and how heritage is a distinctly cultural phenomenon' (2004: 126). From this more subjective point of view, he argues that what constitutes heritage, is 'emic' – based on insider perspectives. Fisher identifies three groups among the local residents in Levuka, who should be involved in the (emic) construction of meaning of this former colonial town. For the ethnic Fijians, history has to do with *vanua*, which is related to the land from where their ancestors originated. This land is not in Levuka, but in another place in Fiji. For this 'original' group of Fijians the colonial buildings of Levuka, which are felt by other groups to be worthy of preservation, do not have intrinsic meaning in their historical consciousness. For the ethnic Fijians places have extra meaning, *mana*, not buildings.

Conversely, a second group – European residents – some of whom are descendents from the colonial occupation but also include new migrants and 'international heritage experts', mark the buildings as historical landmarks. The third group consisting of Indo-Fijians and Chinese shopkeepers represent business interests in the city. They are anxious to protect their businesses from tourism industry outsiders who seek to exploit the heritage of the city. Thus, Ethnic Fijians, old Europeans, Indo-Fijians and Chinese residents should all be included in order to provide a nuanced, hermeneutical, understanding of the heritage of Levuka.

This example illustrates the potential of Hermeneutics in tourism studies. Many more interpretive understandings of tourism are possible in our hybrid network-society where many traditions cross more borders than ever before and create a growing need for mutual interpretations. Hermeneutics has been taken up by a small number of tourism researchers but, so far, with limited influence it would appear. In 2001, Jamal and Hollinshead (2001) identified the hermeneutic or interpretive potentials of qualitative studies of tourism but some 10 years later, writing with a new co-author, Jamal observes that:

> Despite the growing popularity of phenomenology in tourism studies, past attempts have inadequately addressed the theoretical and philosophical assumptions that influence a researcher's approach and interpretations. Furthermore, the potential of hermeneutical phenomenology to address experiential and existential issues related to *being-in-the-world* ... of tourism remains largely unexplored. (Pernecky and Jamal, 2010: 1055, original emphasis)

Hermeneutics are considered here as part of the influence over tourism studies of the 'interpretive turn' within the social sciences. This same 'turn' captures the move by Obenour et al. (2006) to a meaning-based approach (MBA), as an alternative to an information-processing approach (IPA), to quality improvement of tourism services. The MBA investigates how individuals in a cultural context construct their experiences by remembering them as stories. The study employs philosophical hermeneutics (Gadamer, 1972) as a guide to conducting hermeneutics. In another, highly theoretical study, Belhassen and Caton (2009) argues for a linguistic approach to understanding tourism epistemology. This approach clearly includes a prominent role for Hermeneutics.

A last and more concrete example of the hesitant, emerging role of Hermeneutics into the domain of tourism studies comes from Caton and Santos (2008). Guided by post-colonial theory, they interpret photographs taken by students during their Semester at Sea (SAS) study-programme on a cruise-ship that visited many former colonies. In this article a hermeneutical circle (see below) was said to be closed. The circle begins with a pre-figured, post-colonial, gaze that represents places and cultures that the students have internalised through formal and informal education at home. The question posed by the research is whether the photographs taken by the students on the study programme replicate the pre-figured gaze, a question that Caton et al. suggest has had little attention in literature. The photographs were analysed within the framework of hermeneutical theory. The researchers take the position that the photographs are culturally produced, not value-neutral, and are best understood as texts that reflect the discourse of colonialist ideologies. The discussion in the article centres around whether the students' photographs would close or break the hermeneutical circle (see below for further discussion of the hermeneutical circle).

hermeneutics

HISTORICAL DEVELOPMENT

The word 'Hermeneutics' contains the name of the messenger Hermes who translated the divine messages of the Greek gods into the everyday lives of mortals. In this respect Hermeneutics has a long tradition in the exegesis of canonical texts from different eras. It became especially important in the Renaissance Protestant interpretation of the Bible and it remains an important aspect of the humanist study of the ancient classics.

In the interpretation of (holy) texts, a main theme has always been that the meaning of a part can only be understood in relation to the whole. Initially a 'part' might typically be a passage from the Bible or from a book by a Greek or Roman author. Later the 'whole' incorporated a series of generalisations beyond the actual text itself. Consequentially a text had to be placed in its context as a whole, to include the historical context in which the text was written.

The study of interpretations is primarily located in the humanities with its long tradition of the interpretation of texts and has only relatively recently been extended to influence social science. In the social sciences, Phenomenology had a stronger influence on the 'interpretive' turn' (Geertz, 1983) than Hermeneutics. The difference is not always very clear and many links between the two occur. Phenomenology is more concerned with trying to discard all personal judgements (epoche) about the meaning of a phenomenon in order to 'let the situation speak for itself'. In Hermeneutics this type of subjectivity is precisely a point of departure. So for example the 'biases' that psychologists talk of become part of the hermeneutical circles of interpretation, because bias becomes part of the whole that Hermeneutics is trying to understand. A neutral observer would be an absurdity in this interpretive situation because s/he, too, is included in the game of interpretations as a whole.

DESCRIPTION

Through Schleiermacher (1998) and Dilthey (Mul, 2004) in the 19th century and later Heidegger (1972) but especially Gadamer (1972, 1990), Hermeneutics extended its influence far beyond (holy) texts. A premise in Hermeneutics is that in social life it is intuition that helps to assimilate the universe of another human being. Intuitive empathy is complemented by interpretations that are rooted in the background knowledge of the interpreter. The 'experience' (*Erlebnis*) which is at the basis of this understanding is active, full of intention and meaning, and captures the totality of the life of an individual. For example, in the context of conversations about tourism destinations, as in the case of Levuka above, the individuals involved in the dialogue represent 'organic whole beings' from divergent backgrounds. The acceptance of this concept of the whole individual is, what has been labelled in Hermeneutics, as the 'first hermeneutical circle'.

The second circle refers to the relationship between pre-understanding and new understanding. Hermeneutics presumes the existence of pre-understandings of a phenomena. So for example, when we enter a classroom, we have a contextual pre-understanding of the whole situation we are confronted with. It is presumed that in the classroom there are many pre-understandings commonly shared by all people present. Hermeneutics also accepts the 'uncoveredness' of such pre-understandings. When a researcher works in a hermeneutic frame, it is this second hermeneutical circle that they have to step into in order to uncover the (inter)subjectivities that define the group's mutual interpretations.

In any ongoing, hermeneutical research of pre-understanding and understanding, background assumptions are referred to in what Gadamer (1990) calls a *Fragehorizont* – literally 'question-horizon' or questions set in a particular context. A question, asked by a researcher can never be isolated from the much wider horizon or context it is generated from. Consequently, there is a dialectic going on of question and answer that 'das Verstehen als ein Wechselverhältnis von der Art eines Gespräch erscheinen lässt' (Gadamer, 1990: 383), translated here as 'understanding appears like the changing circumstances of a type of conversation'. A new question then develops related to how to understand these horizons and more specifically 'die im Verstehen geschehende Verschmelzung der Horizonte' (fusion of horizons) that Gadamer discusses occur.

The validity of this ongoing understanding through conversation depends on what Gadamer calls 'das wirkungsgeschichtliche Bewusstsein', translated here as 'consciousness related to real historical time'. The consciousness, which contains the results of an actual historical period, would be determined from the ultimate validity of a discourse in a particular era. For example, the same phenomenon, such as romanticism, has been (re)interpreted according to this ongoing changing consciousness since the start of the romantic period to present day. Therefore, this consciousness has a 'logischen Struktur der Offenheit, die das hermeneutische Bewusstsein kennzeichnet' (Gadamer, 1990: 368), meaning that the character of hermeneutical consciousness is to remain open to new interpretations.

POTENTIAL CRITICISM

In Hermeneutics there is a tendency towards relativism and that has often been criticised. Any notion of an objective reality is closed off by hermeneutic circles where the interpreters themselves are imprisoned in their reflections in this 'hall of mirrors' (Geertz, 1983). However, Hermeneutics has been welcomed by (de)constructionist thought and shares its criticisms, which align mostly with this relativist position. An often cited criticism comes from Habermas who refers to the failure of Hermeneutics to acknowledge the power mechanisms that preclude the necessary theoretical sources that people need to understand their situations.

CROSS REFERENCES

Constructionism, Document Analysis, Phenomenology, Repertory Grid.

FURTHER READING

Generic

Gadamer, H. (1972) *Truth and Method*. New York: Crossroad.
Gadamer, H. (1990) *Wahrheit und Methode*. Tübingen: JCB Mohr.
Geertz, C. (1983) *Local Knowledge: Further Essays in Interpretive Anthroplogy*. New York: Basic Books.
Heidegger, M. (1972) *On Time and Being*. New York: Harper & Row.
Mul, de J. (2004) *The Tragedy of Finitude: Dilthey's Hermeneutics of Life*. New Haven, CT: Yale University Press.
Schleiermacher, F. (1998) *Hermeneutics and Criticism and Other Writings*. Cambridge: Cambridge University Press.

Tourism specific

Belhassen, Y. and Caton, K. (2009) Advancing understandings: a linguistic approach to tourism epistemology, *Annals of Tourism Research*, 36 (2): 335–52.
Caton, K. and Santos, C. (2008) Closing the hermeneutic circle photographic encounters with the other, *Annals of Tourism Research*, 35 (1): 7–26.
Fisher, D. (2004) A colonial town for neocolonial tourism, in C.M. Hall and H. Tucker (eds), *Tourism and Post-colonialism: Contested Discourses, Identities and Representations*. London: Routledge, 126–39.

key concepts in tourism research

Jamal, T. and Hollinshead, K. (2001) Tourism and the forbidden zone: the undeserved power of qualitative inquiry, *Tourism Management*, 22 (1): 63–82.

Obenour, W., Patterson, M., Pedersen, P. and Pearson, L. (2006) Conceptualization of a meaning-based research for tourism service experiences, *Tourism Management*, 27 (1): 34–41.

Pernecky, T. and Jamal, T. (2010) (Hermeneutic) phenomenology in tourism studies, *Annals of Tourism Research*, 37 (4): 1055–75.

Interview/Focus Group

> **Definition** A specific form of conversation that seeks to gather information by administering a set of questions.

RELEVANCE

Along with the Survey, the Interview/Focus Group have become the most popular expressions of 'doing' student research projects. If you are interested in gathering insights into your respondents' opinions, perceptions, values and attitudes, then these are very well tried and tested key concepts and there are plenty of examples in the literature to provide best practice advice. Just a small note of caution, do not underestimate the importance of the analysis stage when planning your research project. An aversion to numbers leads many students into imagining that Interviews/Focus Group data will be easier to analyse – not so. In fact, if anything, the more slippery characteristics of language and meaning makes qualitative data slightly more difficult to analyse than quantitative data. Getting some practice on transcribing, sorting and analysing qualitative data before you embark on your own research project is a helpful 'reality check', we have found. It should give you a better, and probably slightly alarming, picture of the time you need to allocate to the data analysis phase of your project.

APPLICATION

The interview is a commonly used data gathering method in tourism research and the following review uses recently published examples to illustrate its use in tourism research rather than attempt a critical analysis. Structured interviews are less common in the literature but Simone-Charteris and Boyd (2010) used them in a study of the role political tourism plays in fostering peace in Northern Ireland and Jager (2010) reports their use in a study of tourism image of a destination, Dullstroom, in South Africa.

The more fluid conversation of a semi-structured interview is of more appeal to researchers working in an interpretivist vein and given the rise in Constructionism it is unsurprising that semi-structured interviews are more popular. Recent examples include Voigt et al.'s (2010) study of wellness tourists, the performative practices of female solo tourists (Jordan, 2008), young peoples' perceptions of fear on holiday (Hughes and Allen, 2010; Mura, 2010) and Irish residents of an English city in respect of diasporic holiday taking. It is often the case that the semi-structured interview is used in conjunction with participant observation as in Weiner et al.'s (2009) study of the marine tour boat employees' attitudes and behaviours associated with marine environment interpretation. An example of interviewing 'couples' as opposed to individuals is provided in Brown and Obenour (2008).

Unstructured or loosely structured interviews are demanding of both the respondent and the researcher in both time and level of engagement. Respondents need to be strongly committed to the subject of the research and Campbell et al.'s (2010) study of volunteers at a national folk festival demonstrates this nicely. Examples of particular forms of analysis of interview data are provided by Buzinde and Santos (2009) in their study of the way tourists decode slave tourism during visits to a plantation. For a broader introduction to interview data analysis we recommend Smith (2010).

Focus groups demand considerable planning in advance and examples of studies involving tourists at destinations are consequentially quite rare (see Uusitalo et al. [2010] on mental maps of Lapland as an exception and Huang Jue and Hsu's [2009] reporting of a 'virtual' focus group of cruise liner passengers). It is much more likely that the respondents will be drawn from the supply side of the tourism industry. Recent examples here include Alexander et al. (2010) on the 'love motel' concept in Taiwan and Cairncross and Buultjens' (2009) study of tourism and hospitality employers' views of Generation Y employees. Resident groups also lend themselves to the focus group as Woosnam et al. (2009) demonstrates in their study of residents' feelings about tourists in their community.

HISTORICAL DEVELOPMENT

The interview has a long standing role in sociological and anthropological research. Researchers at the University of Chicago made extensive use of the interview in their case studies of social life in the 1920s and 1930s. In the social sciences more generally, the rise of Constructionism in the wake of the void left by Positivism in the 1970s heralded a new, and continuing, enthusiasm for the interview.

The focus group is attributed to Robert Merton, Paul Lazarsfeld and colleagues at Columbia University who had used group interviews in America during the Second World War to explore responses to propaganda materials and levels of troop morale, subsequently publishing their work in the 1950s. The technique was further developed as a research tool for consumer behaviour studies. Early applications placed great emphasis on replicating the experimental laboratory and utilised rooms with one-way mirrors to allow covert observation of the group. The technique was later adapted for a range of social research settings: education, health, community development, and the strict environmental conditions for the conduct of a focus group were lifted.

DESCRIPTION

The interview is used in quantitative survey research (see Survey) and in qualitative research. It is the latter form that we concentrate on in this section. The qualitative interview is a special type of conversation in which an interviewer asks questions on a particular topic and carefully listens and records the respondent's answers. The purpose is to understand the meanings attributed to the topic by the respondent. Some commentators refer to the conversation as means to obtain descriptions of the life-world of the interviewee. Interviews are generally conducted on a one-to-one basis. Group interviewing takes the special form of qualitative interviewing called the Focus Group.

Interviews may be structured as in a survey, semi-structured or open-ended in form. The most common form of use in qualitative research is the semi-structured interview. The researcher will develop an interview guide, or *aide-mémoire*, that contains a list of topics or themes to be covered in the interview. The intention is that the themes should all be covered but that the order of questions or the importance given to each theme reflects the ebb and flow of the conversation. In this way the respondents help shape the interview with their responses. In order to hold to a semi-structured form, the interviewer needs to be sensitive to the tasks of following-up lines of thought, or closing down on particular topics and starting new ones. It might also be that the interviewer returns to topics mentioned earlier in the conversation, or probes for a more detailed account of a situation.

Interviews are normally recorded in some way, often with a sound recorder. They are then transcribed and analysed. Transcription is a time consuming process. Analysis might follow the 'constant comparison' technique developed in Grounded Theory or make use of an increasing number of computer packages for qualitative data analysis.

A focus group is an interview process that is designed to uncover insights from a small, usually homogeneous, group of respondents. A moderator creates a non-threatening and permissive environment and directs the conversation using a set of sequenced questions. Participants are encouraged to discuss the topics opened by the moderator and an exchange of views and opinions between members of the group is encouraged. The technique requires additional skills of the moderator over and above those of the interviewer. The moderator must pay careful attention to the direction of the conversation, participant engagement and timing.

Krueger (2004: 393) provides a useful list of research situations in which focus groups have been found to be effective:

- Discovering what prompts particular behaviours.
- Discovering the barriers that impede behaviours.
- Pilot testing of ideas, campaigns, surveys, products and so on.
- Understanding how people feel and think about something, such as a product or service.
- Developing other research instruments such as surveys or case studies.
- Evaluation programmes or products.

Group size varies but around six to eight respondents seem to be commonly used in consumer behaviour and academic research applications. The number of groups needed is determined by the concept of 'saturation' whereby the groups continue to run until the researcher feels there are no new insights presented.

Analysis of focus group discussion is particularly challenging. If focus groups are video recorded, analysis may be undertaken by more than one researcher in order to corroborate findings. Sound tapes are also used but the physical environments in which focus groups are held sometimes militate against a quality recording. In such cases, involving a second researcher acting as a note taker is advised.

POTENTIAL CRITICISM

Critiques of the interview are largely conducted on epistemological grounds – what kind of knowing is provided by interviewing and what kinds of knowledge can be gained from it? As interviews depend on respondent memory recall what reliability checks are available to the researcher? The 'story' is recounted from the respondent's point of view only without researcher observation. There is also the matter of respondents being selective in their memory recall and this also raises questions about the validity of the interview data.

CROSS REFERENCES

Constructionism, Delphi Method, Ethnomethodology, Hermeneutics, Phenomenology, Survey.

FURTHER READING

Generic

Krueger, R.A. (2004) Focus group, in M. Lewis-Beck, R. Bryman and T.F. Liao (eds), *The SAGE Encyclopaedia of Social Science Research Methods*. Thousand Oaks, CA: Sage. pp. 391–5.

Tourism specific

Alexander, M., Chen, C.C., MacLaren, A. and O'Gorman, K.D. (2010) Love motels: oriental phenomenon or emergent sector?, *International Journal of Contemporary Hospitality Management*, 22 (2): 194–208.

Brown, C.A. and Obenour, W.L. (2008) Alcohol's role in creating a leisure subculture and destination mecca: the case of shag dancing, *Annals of Leisure Research*, 11 (3/4): 271–88.

Buzinde, C.N. and Santos, C.A. (2009) Interpreting slave tourism, *Annals of Tourism Research*, 36 (3): 439–58.

Cairncross, G. and Buultjens, J. (2009) Generation Y and work in tourism and hospitality: problem? What problem?, in P. Benckendorff, G. Moscardo and D. Pendergast (eds), *Tourism and Generation Y*. Wallingford: CABI. pp. 143–54.

interview/focus group

123

Campbell, A., Lyons, K., Wearing, S. and Benson, A. (2010) The importance of being valued: solo 'grey nomads' as volunteers at the National Folk Festival, *Annals of Leisure Research*, 12 (3/4): 277–94.

Huang, J. and Hsu, C.H.C. (2009) Interaction among fellow cruise passengers: diverse experiences and impacts, *Journal of Travel & Tourism Marketing*, 26 (5/6): 547–67.

Hughes, H. and Allen, D. (2010) Holidays of the Irish diaspora: the pull of the 'homeland'?, *Current Issues in Tourism*, 13 (1): 1–19.

Jager, A.E. de (2010) How dull is Dullstroom? Exploring the tourism destination image of Dullstroom, *Tourism Geographies*, 12 (3): 349–70.

Jordan, F. (2008) Performing tourism: exploring the productive consumption of tourism in enclavic spaces, *International Journal of Tourism Research*, 10 (4): 293–304.

Mura, P. (2010) 'Scary ... but I like it!' Young tourists' perceptions of fear on holiday, *Journal of Tourism and Cultural Change*, 8 (1/2): 30–49.

Simone-Charteris, M.T. and Boyd, S.W. (2010) Northern Ireland re-emerges from the ashes: the contribution of political tourism towards a more visited and peaceful environment, in O. Moufakkir and I. Kelly (eds), *Tourism, Progress and Peace*. Wallingford: CABI. pp. 179–98.

Smith, S. (2010) *Practical Tourism Research*. Wallingford: CABI.

Uusitalo, M., Fredman, P. and Tyrväinen, L. (2010) Differences in tourists' and local residents' perceptions of tourism landscapes: a case study from Ylläs, Finnish Lapland, *Scandinavian Journal of Hospitality and Tourism*, 10 (3): 310–33.

Voigt, C., Howat, G., Brown, G. and Patterson, I. (2010) Hedonic and eudaimonic experiences among wellness tourists: an exploratory enquiry, *Annals of Leisure Research*, 13 (3): 541–62.

Wiener, C.S., Needham, M.D., Wilkinson, P.F. and Carr, N. (2009) Hawaii's real life marine park: interpretation and impacts of commercial marine tourism in the Hawaiian Islands, *Current Issues in Tourism*, 12 (5/6): 489–504.

Woosnam, K.M., Norman, W.C. and Ying, T.Y. (2009) Exploring the theoretical framework of emotional solidarity between residents and tourists. *Journal of Travel Research*, 48 (2): 245–58.

key concepts in
tourism research

Modelling

Definition A process of creating an abstract and often simplified representation of a system or a phenomenon.

RELEVANCE

If you are tempted to embark on empirical Modelling in your research project then you are likely to have a background in either economics and/ or a substantial training in quantitative methods. If this is not the case then you may find that Modelling tourism, in the empirical tradition, is very challenging. In contrast, conceptual Modelling can provide both a way into and out of a research project. Building a conceptual model from the literature – a visual or literal representation of how previous research-ers have depicted your research topic – can be a useful way to start a research project. Such an approach loosely mimics Deduction, but with-out, necessarily, the generation of hypotheses. Such a model might be better understood as a depiction of the 'sensitising concepts' favoured in Symbolic Interactionism that researchers take into their fieldwork. At the other end of the research process, conceptual models can be constructed from observations and thus provide a useful way to present research find-ings, more than a hint of Grounded Theory influence here.

APPLICATION

Modelling aspects of tourism is a popular strategy for researchers of tourism. Two distinct types of Modelling are to be found: empirical and theoretical. Empirical models are most prevalent in tourism economics and are also common in studies of tourist consumer behaviour. Theoretical or conceptual modelling is applied across a broad range of tourism research topics but especially in studies of tourist behaviour and in tourism planning and policy studies research.

A number of very helpful reviews of empirical Modelling have been published. From two special issues of journals it is possible to grasp the range of empirical modelling in progress. Moutinho and Rita (2006) include articles on forecasting models, econometric models for discrete choice analysis, structural equation modelling, data envelopment analy-sis, decision tables and evolutionary algorithms. In a special issue of *Tourism Economics*, Blake (2008) demonstrates the diversity that is char-acteristic of empirical modelling in tourism in a set of papers that present: an econometric demand model that includes indicators of eco-nomic development, the adoption of econometric tests of willingness to pay for certain tourism attributes, an input–output model in an innova-tive way to provide policy evidence for planning purposes, a theoretical model to explain some of the qualitative features of the tourism area life

modelling

125

cycle model and, finally, an ecological footprint model and a demonstration of how this can be applied to tourism.

The aspiration to achieve explanation and prediction that characterises this work is far from a finished project and many contributions to the literature point to competing claims in Modelling. Song and Li (2008) present a comprehensive review of tourism demand and forecasting modelling since the year 2000 and conclude that 'no single model consistently outperforms other models in all situations'. Consequentially, it is common to find articles that compare and contrast more than one model, examples here include Chen et al. (2008) on forecasting models, Bonn and Harrington (2008) on economic impact models and Shen et al. (2009) on forecasting seasonal demand. Empirical modelling also requires precision in the measurement of variables incorporated into models. Here is another area of ongoing controversy demonstrated by Kozak et al. (2008) in respect of the dependent variable 'tourist spending' and Song et al. (2010) on measures of tourist arrivals and tourist expenditure.

Quantitative empirical models have also been adopted outside of economics. For example, Brida et al. (2010) utilise cluster analysis and multinomial logit modelling to explore the demographic variations in resident perceptions of tourism. In a study of risky destinations Aschauer (2010) sets up independent and dependent variables to measure travellers' characteristics in a perceived unsafe destination. Drawing upon consumer psychology, Bosque and Martin (2008) test a model explaining the interrelationships between psychological variables in tourist satisfaction.

Theoretical modelling based upon the 'models of man' debates in psychology influenced tourist behaviour research in the 1980s (see, for example, Stringer and Pearce, 1984) and continue to influence model building in studies of tourist behaviour (see for example the concept of 'mindfullness' (Moscardo, 1996). A theoretical model in tourism research that has endured for some considerable time is Butler's *Tourism Area Life Cycle Model* (Butler, 2006). Contemporary research has tended to move away from the influences of theoretical disciplinary debates to develop conceptual models of tourism phenomena. So, for example, models are built around topics such as 'greening' (Mair and Jago, 2010), medical tourism (Heung and Kucukusta, 2010) and best practice in community capacity building (Manyara and Jones, 2007). Planning and policy research in tourism has made extensive use of modelling, see for example Zhang and Yan (2009) on power, ideology, interest groups and government influences on tourism policy in China. In something of a twist against this trend Stevenson et al. (2009) have turned back to theory, not to disciplinary but interdisciplinary theory, in their work on complexity theory and tourism policy research.

HISTORICAL DEVELOPMENT

Modelling in the social sciences gained its ascendancy on the back of the general intellectual movement in the mid-20th century to emulate the natural sciences in the pursuit of law-like statements but in this case about human behaviour. While it is certainly true that economics had sought to establish laws for the working of the economy that significantly predate this movement, the general influences of positivism in other social sciences in the 1950s and 1960s, the advances in computational power for handling quantitative data, and the prospects for theorising, explaining and predicting human behaviour proved a heady mix.

The aspiration that sits behind modelling is that it should be possible to establish universal relationships in human behaviour through the observations of constant conjunctions between variables. Variance in behaviour was to be accounted for through scientifically controlled experimentation and modelling was a technique that could handle the complexity of multivariable interactions that characterised the social world. While the social sciences have taken off in other, quite different, directions these aspirations maintain their influence in some social science research communities, see, for example, rational choice theory in sociology and political science and attitude – behaviour studies in social psychology, such as the theory of planned behaviour (Fishbein and Ajzen, 2010).

DESCRIPTION

Two types of models can be found in a broad range of social sciences – Empirical models and Theoretical models. Empirical models seek to demonstrate the relationship between, usually more than one, independent variable and a dependent variable. For example, the relationship between a wide range of social and economic indicators as independent variable and a dependent variable, say, international tourism arrivals in a nation state. Empirical models utilise quantitative data and a range of statistical analysis techniques to test hypotheses about the relationship of the independent variable to, and the strength and direction of that influence over, the dependent variable. Commonly used statistical techniques include discriminant analysis, multiple regression,

modelling

multi-variate analysis such as MANOVA, principle component analysis and cluster analysis. Useful introductory descriptions of these techniques can be found in Lewis-Beck et al. (2004).

In contrast, theoretical models are attempts to show how various forces interact to produce certain phenomenon. They are often depicted diagrammatically and are used to tell a story about real world situations. Theoretical models can be built from data, inductively, or created from the literature, deductively, as a data generating process.

POTENTIAL CRITICISM

Critics of empirical modelling will point to the premises that allow their creation. The presumption that social phenomenon can be reduced to discrete and measurable variables is fundamentally flawed, some will argue. Weaker variants of this line of criticism will focus on the choice of variables, and the measures adopted, to attack the reliability and validity of the models. Others will point to the consistent failure of models to explain sufficient of the variance as a general attack on their contribution to social knowledge production. We would conclude that the early aspirations for modelling in the social sciences that scientific laws might be established around human behaviour have proved somewhat illusory.

Theoretical models have come under attack on two counts. First, they impose a conservative tendency in social enquiry that 'brackets out' more radical thinking about a subject. Consequentially, a self-validating orthodoxy appears that eschews evaluation. Second, they are often attacked as an illusionary form of ordering that produces a guiding fiction about the world as, for example, in some of the arguments about sustainability.

CROSS REFERENCES

Deduction, Empiricism.

FURTHER READING

Generic

Fishbein, M. and Ajzen, I. (2010) *Predicting and Changing Behavior: The Reasoned Action Approach*. New York: Psychology Press.
Lewis-Beck, M., Bryman R. and Liao, T.F. (eds) (2004) *The SAGE Encyclopaedia of Social Science Research Methods*. Thousand Oaks, CA: Sage.

key concepts in tourism research

Tourism specific

Aschauer, W. (2010) Perceptions of tourists at risky destinations. A model of psychological influence factors, *Tourism Review*, 65 (2): 4–20.

Blake, A. (2008) Special section: Economic modelling of tourism, *Tourism Economics*, 14 (4): 669–768.

Bonn, M.A. and Harrington, J. (2008) A comparison of three economic impact models for applied hospitality and tourism research, *Tourism Economics*, 14 (4): 769–89.

Bosque, I.R. del and Martín, H.S. (2008) Tourist satisfaction: a cognitive-affective model, *Annals of Tourism Research*, 35 (2): 551–73.

Brida, J.G., Osti, L. and Barquet, A. (2010) Segmenting resident perceptions towards tourism – a cluster analysis with a multinomial logit model of a mountain community, *International Journal of Tourism Research*, 12 (5): 591–602.

Butler, R.W. (ed.) (2006) *The Tourist Area Life Cycle Volume 2: Conceptual and Theoretical Issues*. Clevedon: Channel View.

Chen, R.J.C., Bloomfield, P. and Cubbage, F.W. (2008) Comparing forecasting models in tourism, *Journal of Hospitality & Tourism Research*, 32 (1): 3–21.

Heung, V.C.S. and Kucukusta, D. (2010) A conceptual model of medical tourism: implications for future research, *Journal of Travel & Tourism Marketing*, 27 (3): 236–51.

Hsu, C.H.C., Cai, L.A. and Li, M. (2010) Expectation, motivation, and attitude: a tourist behavioral model, *Journal of Travel Research*, 49 (3): 282–96.

Kozak, M., Gokovalı, U. and Bahar, O. (2008) Estimating the determinants of tourist spending: a comparison of four models, *Tourism Analysis*, 13 (2): 143–55.

Mair, J. and Jago, L. (2010) The development of a conceptual model of greening in the business events tourism sector, *Journal of Sustainable Tourism*, 18 (1): 77–94.

Manyara, G. and Jones, E. (2007) Best practice model for community capacity-building: a case study of community-based tourism enterprises in Kenya, *Tourism* (Zagreb), 55 (4): 403–15.

Moscardo, G. (1996) Mindful visitors, *Annals of Tourism Research*, 23 (2): 376–97.

Moutinho, L. and Rita, P. (2006) Special issue: New quantitative models in travel and tourism research, *Journal of Travel & Tourism Marketing*, 21 (4): 1–137.

Shen, S., Li, G. and Song H.Y. (2009) Effect of seasonality treatment on the forecasting performance of tourism demand models, *Tourism Economics*, 15 (4): 693–708.

Song, H.Y. and Li, G. (2008) UK Tourism demand modelling and forecasting – a review of recent research, *Tourism Management*, 29 (2): 203–20.

Song, H.Y., Li, G., Witt, S.F., Fei, B.G., Blake, A. and Cortés-Jiménez, I. (2010) Tourism demand modelling and forecasting: how should demand be measured?, *Tourism Economics*, 16 (1): 63–81.

Stevenson, N., Airey, D. and Miller, G. (2009) Complexity theory and tourism policy research, *International Journal of Tourism Policy*, 2 (3): 206–20.

Stringer, P. and Pearce, P.L. (1984) Towards a symbiosis of social psychology and tourism studies, *Annals of Tourism Research*, 11: 5–17.

Zhang, H.Q.Q. and Yan, Q. (2009) The effects of power, ideology, interest groups, and the government on tourism policy making – a conceptual model, *Journal of China Tourism Research*, 5 (2): 158–73.

modelling

129

Narrative

> **Definition** A narrative approach sees storytelling as a promising new, qualitative approach to the understanding of subtle questions of identity, life history and social dynamics.

RELEVANCE

Telling and recording 'stories' is gaining ground as a legitimate form of enquiry in tourism research. This can either be in the form of respondents' stories or in the representation of stories in literature, film, art, music, photography – in fact – in a whole range of what are called expressions of material culture. These research practices are founded upon the key concept of Narrative. The rise of Narrative is not without its detractors however and if you do choose it then you need to be aware that it is likely to attract serious criticism, particularly on validity and reliability grounds. These, and the likely gut reactions of your student mates in the pub that storytelling can be a legitimate form of research should not put you off exploring this key concept because there are sensible answers to both sets of detractors.

APPLICATION

Tourists and tourist professionals all have stories to tell of their own and others' experiences and behaviours and the potential for narrative analysis seems endless. We begin with two examples to demonstrate different uses of Narrative analysis; the story of family holidays (Gram, 2005), and the application of narrative analysis to tourism management (Obenour et al., 2006). Gram (2005) explores the experiences of family holidays with young children and uses narrative to capture 'good' moments on holiday, the opportunities and constraints experienced by families with young children and the influence of specific tourism contexts. There is also a useful and detailed exploration of narrative as a form of qualitative research. Obenour and colleagues turn their tourists' narratives into a managerial intervention to improve the quality of services but they are cautiously mindful of the inherent incompleteness, contextuality and ambiguity of narrative accounts (see also Riessman, 1993).

Narrative analysis can combine both text and image to good effect in the study of destination image. For example, Santos (2004) describes the different frames of Portugal (contemporary and traditional) which are represented by narratives such as 'Romanticised perceptions and implications of the past' or 'Urban Portugal'. The life histories of post-retirement tourists provide rich stories of the social meaning of holidays for Nimrod (2008) in his study of the lifelong interests, leisure activities and social networks of travelling retirees during the 10 years after their retirement. Backpackers' culture, too, is impregnated with narrative accounts. An example is Noy's (2004) exploration of the socio-cultural context of narrative, in this case of contemporary Israeli culture, against which the self-changing narratives of backpackers construct a collective notion of identity. This line of research suggests a rich environment of interpersonal communication, in which storytelling frequently occurs and through which the social construction of identity is pursued.

Narrative research has also been employed to research contentious cultural heritage. An interesting example is the Gettysburg storyscape, that illustrates the way in which a text is co-constructed by both marketeers and consumers, through negotiation and embodied performance (Chronis, 2005). Examining tourism through a mutually constructive process between producers and consumers has been, to a large extent, under-investigated, according to this author and narrative analysis provides a way into these interactions. In the example of an American Civil War battle, Chronis shows how a landscape is 'symbolically transformed and used by service providers and tourists alike to negotiate, define and strengthen social values of patriotism and national unity, "in times when these values are most needed"' (Chronis, 2005: 386).

Individually written narratives of domestic Korean students, who visited sacred places in Korea, have been evaluated in order to examine the symbolic interrelationships between heritage tourism and national identity (Hyung yu Park, 2010). Nuance uses travel narratives from 1835 to 1870 to reconstruct how and why local people 'retained considerable personal autonomy and control over tourism business many centuries old' (2007: 1060) and to show that Western tourists were interested in Ottoman heritage before Cook Company tours began in 1869. In Mordue (2005) it can be seen that narratives were used in power games of cultural heritage, for example in tactics of social exclusion in a central tourist district of the city of York.

A different narrative research question has been posed by Yan and Santos (2009), 'how does the Other represent itself in tourism discourse?' According to the authors of the study a tourism promotional video 'China forever' conforms to an Orientalist discourse by:

1   revealing a changeless, nostalgic and feminised China that speaks to a Western Orientalist imagination; and
2   creating a modern China subjugated to Western understanding and authority over modernity.

Here, the authors conclude, the (Chinese) Other represents itself by self-Orientalism.

Narratives have also been used in self-reflective accounts of tourism research. Ren et al. (2010) locate narratives within actor-network theory. The published narratives of the three authors of this study seek to show how knowledge is constantly ordered and orchestrated within the multiple networks and voices of the tourism academy. Echtner (1999) applied semiotics – 'a science that studies signs within society' (Saussure, 1916 [1966]: 16) – to tourism research, focusing on marketing studies.

HISTORICAL DEVELOPMENT

Narratology (Bal, 1997) is the theory of narratives, narrative texts, images, spectacles, events and cultural artefacts that 'tell a story'. Such a theory can help researchers understand, analyse and evaluate narratives. It analyses texts by using categories such as; different types of narrator, focalised subject and object, changing perspectives, levels of narration, indirect speech, and the relationships between primary and embedded texts. Narrative analysis originated in the field of literary criticism, but, as Geertz stated in 1983 in his idea of 'blurred genres' in which he challenged anthropology and literary criticism to cooperate, the narrative approach has now entered the social sciences. Many academics – Appadurai, Bal, Bakhtin, Barthes, Baudrillard, Bhabha, Clifford, Derrida, Geertz, Lévi-Strauss, Ricoeur and Saïd – have been involved in interdisciplinary efforts to translate the narrative approach from the humanities into the social sciences. For example, Bakhtin developed the notion that language use – or rather discourse – is 'always an intertwining of different discourses coming from a variety of backgrounds. This is known as the dialogic principle' (Bal, 1997: 64) and it lies behind the much discussed 'interpretive turn' in the social sciences.

Clifford and Marcus (1986) introduced the dialogic principle into anthropology by conceiving the ethnographer in conversation with 'natives' of a culture. The writings of anthropologists are seen as an 'interlocution' *with* instead of *from* natives. In his polyphonic model many voices need to be interpretively attuned in accordance with this basic principle. In his view the collage functions as a constructivist assemblage that contains voices other than the ethnographer's and data not fully co-terminus with the governing interpretation. Here, too, storytelling contributes to giving voice to these subordinate interpretations. By telling the stories of their lives people construct identities, helping students of the biographical method to not only study persons, but also social collectives, including societies and corporations, to which these persons are connected.

DESCRIPTION

According to Barthes, who sees a central role for the narrative in social life, 'Caring nothing for the division between good and bad literature, narrative is international, trans-historical, trans-cultural: it is simply there, like life itself' (1977: 79).

The value of storytelling as an approach to extracting new meanings and new learning has now been well established (McDrury and Alterio, 2003). As a method, it can lead to increased insights and knowledge for both the listener and the teller. It is deeply grounded within the cultural context in which stories are told, for example through the plot, the voices, performance action, personality of the teller and perspective of the audience. Therefore it allows humans to create negotiated transactions of knowledge and perception. It builds a knowledge base of conceptual narrative frameworks that inform the social condition.

Following the narratology of Bal (1997), we can speak of narrative texts (a text in which an agent relates a story in a particular medium) of a story presented in a certain manner (a series of logically and chronologically related events that are caused or experienced by actors) of an event (transition from one state to the other). The translation of his narratology into tourism research deserves further work.

POTENTIAL CRITICISM

The adoption of narrative analysis is not without its detractors. Czarniawska puts it this way: 'But worries about the status of the narrative material are relatively small compared to the worries about "narrativized" social science. Does anything go in social science writing?' (2004: 132). Tourism researchers who apply narrative analysis will heed Czarniawska's warning and have to deal with the strong reactions against the postmodernist predilection summarised as 'Anything goes' (Feyerabend, 1975). The justification of narrative research as a contributor to social knowledge will have to answer the question, 'What is good narrative research?' if it is to compete effectively as a methodology in the social sciences. This, again, points to a recurrent theme in this book, that our key concepts are subject to a long standing debate in social sciences on the possibilities of a 'science' inspired by both the natural sciences and the humanities.

CROSS REFERENCES

Constructionism, Hermeneutics, Phenomenology.

FURTHER READING

Generic

Bal, M. (1997) *Narratology: Introduction to the Theory of Narrative*. Toronto: University of Toronto.
Barthes, R. (1977) *Mythologies*. France: Edition de Seuil.
Clifford, J. and Marcus, G.E. (eds) (1986) *Writing Culture. The Poetics and Politics of Ethnography*. Berkeley, CA: University of California Press.
Czarniawska, B. (2004) *Narratives in Social Science Research. Introducing Qualitative Methods*. London: Sage.
Feyerabend, P. (1975) *Against Method*. London: NLB.
Geertz, C. (1983) *Local Knowledge: Further Essays in Interpretive Anthropology*. New York: Basic Books.
McDrury, J. and Alterio, M. (2003) *Learning through Storytelling in Higher Education*. London: Sage.
Riessman, C. (1993) *Narrative Analysis*. London: Sage.
Saussure, F. (1916/1966) *Course in General Linguistics*. New York: McGraw-Hill.

Tourism specific

Chronis, A. (2005) Co-constructing heritage at the Gettysburg storyscape, *Annals of Tourism Research*, 32 (2): 386–406.
Echtner, C. (1999) The semiotic paradigm: implications for tourism research, *Tourism Management*, 20 (1): 47–57.
Gram, M. (2005) Family holidays: a qualitative analysis of family holiday experiences, *Scandinavian Journal of Hospitality and Tourism*, 1: 12–22.
Hyung yu Park (2010) Emotional journeys in nationhood, *Annals of Tourism Research*, 37 (1): 116–35.

Mordue, T. (2005) Tourism performance and social exclusion in 'Olde York', *Annals of Tourism Research*, 32 (1): 179–198.

Nimrod, G. (2008) Retirement and tourism: themes in retirees narratives, *Annals of Tourism Research*, 35 (4): 859–78.

Noy, C. (2004) This trip really changed me: backpackers' narratives of self-change, *Annals of Tourism Research*, 31 (1): 78–102.

Nuance, S. (2007) A facilitated access model and Ottoman empire tourism, *Annals of Tourism Research*, 34 (4): 1056–1077.

Obenour, W., Patterson, M., Pedersen, P. and Pearson, L. (2006) Conceptualisation of a meaning-based approach for tourism service experiences, *Tourism Management*, 27 (1): 34–41.

Ren, C., Pritchard, A. and Morgan, N. (2010) Constructing tourism research: a critical inquiry, *Annals of Tourism Research*, 37 (4): 885–904.

Santos, C. (2004) Framing Portugal representation dynamics, *Annals of Tourism Research*, 31 (2): 112–38.

Yan, G. and Santos, C. (2009) 'China forever': tourism discourse and self-orientalism, *Annals of Tourism Research*, 36 (2): 295–315.

Paradigm

Definition 'Some accepted examples of actual scientific practice – laws, theories, applications, and instrumentation taken together – providing models from which spring particular coherent traditions of scientific research' (Kuhn, 1962: 10). Without paradigms there would simply be no way of practising science.

paradigm

RELEVANCE

This is 'a must read' key concept because Kuhn's ideas provided such an important counterpoint to Popper's thesis in shaping ideas about scientific knowledge production. It is also often used in the tourism research literature, but as we argue below, in ways that verge on misuse. An understanding of the original meaning of the concept and its reinterpretation in contemporary tourism research can increase your self-understanding of the identity of the research selections you are trying to make.

APPLICATION

In tourism studies, as in the rest of social science, the concept of a paradigm has come to be used in a wide variety of ways. In 'The truth about tourism' Tribe (2006) explores the congruence between the canon of tourism knowledge and its phenomenal world from a social-constructionist approach. In his analysis he accentuates the use of a claim of Paradigm status as a defence mechanism of its adherents against emerging subversive theories, because paradigms set the rules and define the boundaries of research during a period of normal science. Tribe distinguishes between current times, described as postmodern, and Kuhn's era. Commenting on the time in which Kuhn was writing, Tribe observes that 'patronage and the monopolization of knowledge were rife and the communication of ideas was tightly controlled' (Tribe, 2006: 366). Arguing that the present era is quite different Tribe rejects the Paradigm as a suitable concept for understanding contemporary tourism research, claiming that different 'traditions' may 'freely co-exist and are more permeable and adaptable' (Tribe, 2006: 366).

We would largely agree with Tribe and suggest that a comparison with Kuhn's pre-paradigmatic phase in which different schools compete, seems a more appropriate way to describe the correct application of the concept of Paradigm in tourism research in the early 21st century. This was the argument followed by Riley and Love (2000) in their article about an 'interpretive Paradigm' as a necessary concept to support qualitative data analyses in tourism research. Here, they are exemplifying Tribe's assertion of a defence mechanism as they try to carve out a space for qualitative research in the face of the (then) dominance of quantitative research in tourism research because, Riley and Love argue, the tourism industry is 'economically driven and thus has a clear place for quantification' (2000: 176). However, they claim that a 'paradigm shift took place that resulted in a variety of qualitative methods'. In our view the word Paradigm has not been chosen well, though, because later the dominant, positivistic paradigm was distinguished from an emergent, naturalistic one supporting qualitative research. A Paradigm shift in a Kuhnian sense would imply the future dominance of the qualitative paradigm. In our view the article better reflects discussion typical of a pre-paradigmatic period, where schools of thought compete for dominance. We suggest therefore that even where authors earnestly engage with the concept of Kuhn's Paradigm, confusion reigns as to its true meaning. We would acknowledge that since Kuhn's original thesis was published, his concept has been used in very many more ways than he intended, furthermore that the scientific community has become somehow used to this confusion. We try to demonstrate how this confusion is played out in the tourism literature below.

The concept has been used in relation to the establishment of a 'planning Paradigm' for tourism (Alipour, 1996), as a 'semiotic Paradigm' to suggest directions for future tourism research (Echtner, 1999), as an over-arching versus inflexible legitimation of an emergent tradition of thought about sustainability or as a suggestion of unity where fuzziness reigns (Hunter, 1997; Saarinen, 2006), and as a 'host-guest Paradigm' (Aramberri, 2001). Li (2008) uses the 'variable Paradigm' in support of a view that there are abundant opportunities to explore the field of entrepreneurship and Stone and Sharpley (2008) present an extended 'thanatological Paradigm', which offers a model of dark tourism for further theoretical and empirical analysis with an exploration of the demand side of dark tourism.

Paradigms can be 'revised' as in Dunlop's alternative 'agricultural Paradigm' that allows for the necessary gender differences in agro-tourism (McGehee et al., 2007), as a 'conflict Paradigm' – a type of relationship between stakeholders – that 'evaluates' the relationship between tourism and cultural heritage in Hong Kong (McKercher et al., 2005), as the widely accepted 'eclectic Paradigm' of international production as explaining the various motives for foreign investment in tourism (Dwyer and Forsyth, 1994), as a Paradigm for China's red tourism (Huimin et al., 2007).

It seems that more and more researchers seek to legitimise a particular domain of studies through the concept of a Paradigm, for example wildlife tourism (Rodger et al., 2009), tourism and hospitality development (Hegarty, 1992), the consumer's reactions to a tourist attraction (Mazursky, 1989), postmodernism (Andereck, 2006), a personal guide-tourist relationship (Cohen et al., 2002) and many others. The contemporary use of the term Paradigm in the tourism literature is very far removed from Kuhn's intentions in 1962. Such diversity of use of term worries some, as McFee's comments suggest, 'within social science the concept of a Paradigm is less useful, because there exists a wide range of competing, and complementary perspectives ...' (2007: 61).

paradigm

HISTORICAL DEVELOPMENT

It remains an interesting challenge to study the similarities and differences between different accounts of knowledge production. Concepts like the 'language games' of Wittgenstein, the 'universes of discourse' of

Mannheim, the 'frames of reference' of C. Wright Mills, the power-knowledge constellations of Foucault might be very usefully compared to the 'paradigms' of Kuhn (1962). Kuhn's major contribution, however, was to propose that research is impossible without a Paradigm that determines what constitutes a theory or a fact. This is evidenced by a shared consensus and commitment to the same rules and standards for scientific practices. However, the whole idea of a paradigm has never been very clear right from its entry into scientific debate. For example, Margaret Masterman (1970), who sympathised with Kuhn, counted no fewer than 21 different senses of the concept in his (1962) book. Thus a lack of precision and evident vagueness of the concept from the start has probably been the reason for the multitude of meanings that have followed in more recent times.

In the social sciences, Kuhn's ideas have been received with more enthusiasm than in the natural sciences. This, despite the observation that there has never been a Paradigm in the social sciences that would equate to the 'normal science' of Darwin, Newton and others in the field of the natural sciences that were in Kuhn's sights as he proposed his thesis. During the 1970s (neo-)Marxism, structural-functionalism, symbolic interactionism, figurational sociology, just to mention some of the pre-paradigmatic schools in sociology, wholeheartedly embraced the idea of a paradigm, that would support the scientific status of their own theoretical frame. From another direction and quite as Kuhn might have predicted as symptomatic of a pre-paradigmatic period in the social sciences, so-called empiricists gathered facts at random and in the best cases proposed empirical generalisations as a 'theoretical framework'. This cleavage between the theoretical and empirical tradition in social sciences has never been solved and the use of the concept of a Paradigm made it even more diffuse than ever (Masterman, 1970).

More recently, social scientists use the word 'Paradigm' as a sort of a container-concept for new theories and empirical generalisations, especially in relatively new fields of knowledge such as management or communication studies. The word has also entered everyday usage to indicate that some new insight has emerged and so a new fashion, a hype, a model, or a thought, can be called paradigmatic in order to establish its legitimacy.

DESCRIPTION

Thomas Kuhn made a distinction between periods of normal and abnormal science in the history of the natural sciences of modern times. In periods of normal science, research is based on scientific examples of the

key concepts in tourism research

past that are considered the heritage of the fundamentals for scientific practice. The example set by Newton served as such a paradigm for centuries. Without such a Paradigm any theoretical development is only ever partial and competes with many others. Consequentially the gathering of facts is a rather random activity. Divergent interpretations in various pre-paradigmatic schools dictate the fields of study in this process of pre-scientific knowledge production. The endeavours become scientific when one Paradigm has been established after its victory over the others. During a period of normal science the theories developed with the Paradigm are tested. Scientists are trained to emulate a particular tradition within theory and to apply the methods that are used to do research within the framework of these theories. Thus under the conditions of normal science what is tested, Kuhn argued, is not so much the theory but more the capacity of the researcher to undertake research.

Kuhn calls this 'puzzle solving' instead of the testing of theories. Such a period of normal science only changes into another one through a short and intense period of abnormal science in which different paradigms struggle for their existence. One wins out and becomes the new paradigm in a new period of normal science. This image of how scientific development takes place has been much discussed since Kuhn (1962) published his book. The crux of the argument is that the growth of knowledge does not take place according to well defined scientific criteria such as falsification, but has to be related to developments in a wider, non-scientific context during periods of abnormal science. Popper's thesis that the growth of scientific knowledge can be understood as an internal process based on falsification was, therefore, rejected by Kuhn and many would argue that it opens up the field of social science to a further pre-paradigmatic phase.

It is worth, here, referring the reader to Smith and Lee's (2010) analysis of the use of theory in tourism research. In this book chapter the authors present an interesting discussion on the use of the term theory in the tourism literature and using a set of criteria they create seven categories of use. In the light of the Kuhn/Popper debate we describe above, the finding that Smith and Lee come to at the close of their chapter raises an interesting angle on the matter of a Paradigm in tourism research. Following their analysis they conclude, 'Still, we suggest that 'theory', in a published research context, should be limited to Type 1 and Type 2 theory. In other words, 'theory' is most appropriately used in the context of models that are based on substantial empirical evidence and that produce falsifiable predictions' (Smith and Lee, 2010: 11). In order to come to such a view we would argue that these authors have used their chapter to reinforce a Popperian view of 'normal' science in tourism research. A view that we would suggest is but one of many positions, or traditions, that are fighting for dominance in an abnormal pre-paradigmatic period for the social sciences and, consequentially, within tourism research as well.

POTENTIAL CRITICISM

The most important critique of Kuhn still comes from that launched by Popper in a landmark publication that included exchanges between Kuhn and Popper (Lakatos and Musgrave, 1970). According to Popper a distinction should be drawn between first class research – pure science – and between second class, applied research where scientists mainly are involved in the 'puzzle solving', as Kuhn described it. Pure science deals with 'real problems' instead of puzzles to be solved. In this respect there have always been competing theories that are entangled in a serious scientific struggle to solve 'real' problems. For Popper there is an inner logic of scientific growth and it is not fruitful to be oriented towards marginal (applied, second class) sciences like sociology and psychology in order to explain the growth of scientific knowledge (Lakatos and Musgrave, 1970: 51–9). A social psychologist once showed Popper his psychological study on the group processes in a chemical laboratory in order to explain how this research evolved. Popper's reaction was along the lines of what on earth was this research about? (Popper, 1976).

Other critiques of Kuhn relate to the way in which he proposed to understand what happens in periods of abnormal science. According to various authors one might also include power analysis (Foucault, 1969, 1975; Bourdieu 2004), sociological analysis (Elias, 1987) or analyse in more depth actually what happens in scientific laboratories (Latour, 1987).

CROSS REFERENCES

Constructionism, Deduction, Postmodernism.

FURTHER READING

Generic

Bourdieu, P. (2004) *Science of Science and Reflexivity*. Cambridge: Polity Press.
Elias, N. (1987) *Involvement and Detachment: Contributions to the Sociology of Knowledge*. Oxford: Blackwell.

Kuhn, T.S. (1962) *The Structure of Scientific Revolutions*. Chicago: The University of Chicago.

Lakatos, I. and Musgrave, A. (1970) *Criticism and The Growth of Knowledge*. Cambridge: Cambridge University Press.

Masterman, M. (1970) The nature of a paradigm, in I. Lakatos and A. Musgrave (eds), *Criticism and the Growth of Knowledge*. Cambridge: Cambridge University Press. pp. 59–89.

Foucault, M. (1969) *L'árchéologie du savoir*. Paris: Gallimard.

Foucault, M. (1975) *Surveiller et punir*. Paris: Gallimard.

Latour, B. (1987) *Science in Action*. Cambridge, MA: Harvard University Press.

Popper, Sir K.R. (1976) *Unended Quest: An Intellectual Autobiography*. London, Routledge.

Tourism specific

Alipour, H. (1996) Tourism development within planning paradigm: the case of Turkey, *Tourism Management*, 17 (5): 367–77.

Andereck, K. (2006) Film-induced tourism, *Annals of Tourism Research*, 33 (1): 278–80.

Aramberri, J. (2001) The host should get lost: paradigms in the tourism theory, *Annals of Tourism Research*, 28 (3): 738–61.

Cohen, E., Ifergan, M. and Cohen, E. (2002) A new paradigm in guiding: the Madrich as a new role, *Annals of Tourism Research*, 29 (4): 919–32.

Dwyer, L. and Forsyth, P. (1994) Foreign tourism investment: motivation and impact, *Annals of Tourism Research*, 21 (3): 512–37.

Echtner, C. (1999) The semiotic paradigm: implications for tourism research, *Tourism Management*, 20 (1): 47–57.

Hegarty, J. (1992) Towards establishing a new paradigm for tourism and hospitality development, *International Journal of Hospitality Management*, 11 (4): 309–17.

Huimin, G., Ryan, C. and Wei, Z. (2007) Jinggangshan mountain. A paradigm of China's red tourism, in C. Ryan (ed.), *Battlefield Tourism: History, Place, Interpretation*. Amsterdam: Elsevier. pp. 59–65.

Hunter, C. (1997) Sustainable tourism as an adaptive paradigm, *Annals of Tourism Research*, 24 (4): 850–67.

Li, L. (2008) A review of entrepreneurship research published in the hospitality and tourism management journals, *Tourism Management*, 29 (5): 1013–22.

Mazursky, D. (1989) Past experience and future tourism decisions, *Annals of Tourism Research*, 16 (3): 333–44.

McFee, G. (2007) Paradigms and possibilities. Or some concerns for the study of sport from the philosophy of science, *Sports, Ethics and Philosophy*, 1 (1): 58–77.

McGehee, N., Kim, K. and Jennings, G. (2007) Gender and motivation for agri-tourism entrepreneurship, *Tourism Management*, 28 (1): 280–9.

McKercher, B., Ho, P. and du Cros, H. (2005) Relationships between tourism and cultural heritage management: evidence from Hong Kong, *Tourism Management*, 26 (4): 539–48.

Riley, R. and Love, L. (2000) The state of qualitative tourism research, *Annals of Tourism Research*, 27 (1): 164–87.

paradigm

Rodger, K., Moore, S. and Newsome, D. (2009) Wildlife tourism, science and actor network theory, *Annals of Tourism Research*, 36 (4): 645–66.

Saarinen, J. (2006) Traditions of sustainability in tourism studies, *Annals of Tourism Research*, 330 (4): 1121–40.

Smith, S. and Lee, H. (2010) A typology of 'theory' in tourism, in D. Pearce and R. Butler (eds) *Tourism Research: A 20–20 Vision*. Oxford: Goodfellow Publishers, pp. 28–42.

Stone, P. and Sharpley, R. (2008) Consuming dark tourism: a thanatological perspective, *Annals of Tourism Research*, 35 (2): 574–95.

Tribe, J. (2006) The truth about tourism, *Annals of Tourism Research*, 33 (2): 360–81.

Phenomenology

Definition A scientific approach to the world developed in the humanities as a response to the empiricist traditions of the natural sciences and its imitations in social science. It is an approach to know the world through direct experiences of phenomena, first developed by the philosopher and mathematician Edmund Husserl (1859–1938). Phenomenology tries to deduce essential characteristics, through reasoned inquiry which discovers the inherent essence of appearance (Stewart, 1990).

RELEVANCE

If you have research interests in aspects of 'experience' then reading about phenomenology is a must. The application of phenomenological inquiry, however, can take many forms and wide reading outside tourism studies in education, medicine, psychology and religion, is strongly advised.

APPLICATION

Phenomenology as a methodology has been largely overlooked in tourism research (Dann and Cohen, 1996). Nevertheless, the theoretical and rather speculative article by Cohen (1979), 'A phenomenology of tourist experiences' has been influential for many researchers (Yiping Li, 2000: 864). In his article, Cohen asked himself what tourists were looking for and he distinguished five modes of experience during the tourist journey, as a phenomenological answer to that question. The general idea behind these modes was that each individual has to conform to some extent to the pressures from society. The subsequent feelings of tension and discontent are temporarily relieved through tourism and recreation. The first two types (modes) represent a pleasant escape from everyday life, whereas in the other three, people look for some 'valuable elements of the world outside everyday life'. The introduction of more sophisticated thoughts about extension or escape from the alienation in everyday life, Cohen meant his categorisation as a 'theoretical baseline for more profound empirical studies of tourist experiences' (1979: 198). In this categorisation he referred heavily to the concept of 'finite provinces of meaning separate from reality, though this is not explicitly admitted by either the tourists or the staff of tourist establishments' (Cohen, 1979: 184). His theoretical inspiration comes from the phenomenology of Schütz and Luckmann (1973). Variation in different types of tourism seem to be recognised with this model, stemming from a crucial characteristic of the additional value of the phenomenological method, in its intention to let the situation speak for itself.

Yiping Li (2000) studied the consciousness arising from the spatial and temporal bonds between people and places. He described the lived experience of Canadian tourists travelling to and within China and discussed if and how geographical consciousness influenced tourists' experiences. The focus of this study was on people's life-worlds (see later) including geographical consciousness, in which 'everyone is a geographer in a world practically geographical' (Lowenthal, 1961). This study is a good example of how the phenomenological method can be used in tourism research. Other studies adopting a phenomenological framework are: Masberg and Silverman (1996) who examined college students' experiences at heritage sites; Lengkeek (1996) whose study illustrated that experiences vary over time; Reichel et al. (2005) who studied the types of experiences of Israeli backpackers; and Hayllard and Griffin (2005) who investigated the nature of the tourist experience in the Rocks historic precinct of Sydney.

Andriotis (2009) reported a phenomenological study of the visitor experience at the mount of Athos, a sacred site experience. This study nicely demonstrates Cohen's existential category because it introduces a spiritual perspective. Jamal and Hollinshead (2001) make a plea for a clear choice in favour of an interpretive approach in tourism academia, phenomenology being an important part of such an approach. In this unparalleled age of cultural diffusion, tourism interpretations are more influential than ever in their constructive power. Therefore, tourism research needs to take this promising, subjective and meaningful richness into an interpretive account. Selby's (2004) work on the urban tourist experience and Selby et al. (2010) on tourism and the fear of crime, both incorporate a Schutzian dimension (see below for description of Schütz).

HISTORICAL DEVELOPMENT

Phenomenology is not knowledge in the usual meaning of the word, but intuition as opposed to scientific knowledge of natural sciences. The phenomenological method (*Wesenschau*) is an internal, intellectual explaining of the object, as it is described in this intellectual process and not as an object external to the consciousness. Edmund Husserl (1965) resisted empiricism as well as rationalism and wanted to allow a phenomenon to speak for itself by trying to purify our consciousness from pre-judgements regarding these phenomena. He wanted an unprejudiced approach of the world without any interpretation in advance. In this approach the subject does not focus on a research-object but on the structure of her/his own thinking in relation to an object. Consciousness, for Husserl, is always consciousness of something (the intentionality of the consciousness). Therefore, its essential task is to produce clear, precise and systematic descriptions of meaning (with their underlying worldviews) constituting the activity of consciousness in human experience. Later Husserl's attention switched from consciousness, to the life-world, which is the whole self-evidence marking our experience. Other philosophers, for example, Merleau-Ponty, Sartre and Heidegger, have been influenced by Husserl. In social science and the humanities especially, Alfred Schütz is the most influential proponent of the phenomenological approach.

For Schütz (Schütz and Luckmann 1973), the experiences in one's life-world are crucial in our understanding of the world. Schütz and Luckmann (1973: 36) concentrated on the structure of the common-sense world of everyday life. For Schütz 'the reality of everyday life is organized around the "here" of my body and the "now" of my present. This "here and now" is the focus of my attention to the reality of everyday life' (1973: 36). In this 'here and now', actions of different people are reciprocally typified and a structure will be created in everyday life that remains self-evident unless one is forced to break out of this 'finite province of meaning' into another one. In such a situation a wide-awake and 'normal' adult taking his surrounding world for granted, would be disturbed by 'foreign' interference, through experiencing a specific shock, exploding the limits of what is for him a momentary 'real', what we might call 'culture shock'. Schütz's writings have greatly influenced phenomenological theorising and research in the social sciences.

Through the phenomenological analysis of social reality, social science and the humanities reach a level of sophistication previously thought impossible under positivist explanations in an empiricist tradition. Combined with the hermeneutical and pragmatist traditions of Symbolic Interactionism in sociology (see Denzin, 1992), psychology, or symbolic anthropology, phenomenology has contributed much to the 'interpretive turn' in social science. Phenomenology circles around the interpretations of meaningful actions in people's everyday life. It has helped shift the dominant goal of social science from the explanation of the social world to an emphasis on understanding.

DESCRIPTION

Through an unprejudiced approach Husserl wanted to attain an eidetical (*eidos* = original image) reduction of the world (Polkinghorne, 1989). Through the *Eidetische Reduktion* all scientific and non-scientific experiences, judgements, sentences, appreciations, etc. related to a specific object in reality are ruled out and as a result, the essence of this object becomes free and can be understood. So, instead of using questionnaires to record people's behaviour in a tourist attraction, one could decide to sit in the attraction without any pre-judgement and let the situation speak for itself. Gradually, patterns of visitor behaviour would emerge that could not be understood from the questionnaire responses. The situation in the tourist attraction speaks for itself when the pre-formed judgements of a questionnaire are ruled out and the essence of the tourist attraction become freely understood.

POTENTIAL CRITICISM

Although Husserl claimed his phenomenology to be a method beyond idealism and materialism, it has been criticised because of its subjective idealism. Its accent on an intentional consciousness and its alliance with other 'interpretive' traditions has lead to a strong criticism by the positivist, empiricist tradition in social science.

CROSS REFERENCES

Constructionism, Hermeneutics.

FURTHER READING

Generic

Denzin, N.K. (1992) *Symbolic Interactionism and Cultural Studies: The Politics of Interpretation.* Oxford: Blackwell.

Husserl, E. (1965) *Philosophie als strenge Wissenschaft (1910–1911).* Frankfurt am Main: Vittorio Klostermann.

Merleau-Ponty, M. (1962) What is phenomenology?, *Cross Currents*, 6: 59–70.

Polkinghorne, D.E. (1989) Phenomenological research methods, in R.S. Valle and S. Halling (eds), *Existential-Phenomenological Perspectives in Psychology: Exploring the Breadth of Human Experience.* New York: Plenum. pp. 41–62.

Schütz, A. and Luckmann, T. (1973) *The Structures of the Life-World.* London: Heinemann.

Stewart, D. (1990) *Exploring Phenomenology. A Guide to the Field and Literature.* Athens, OH: Ohio University Press.

Tourism specific

Andriotis, K. (2009) Sacred site experience: a phenomenological study, *Annals of Tourism Research*, 36 (1): 64–84.

Cohen, E. (1979) A phenomenology of the tourist experiences, *Sociology*, 13 (2): 179–201.

Dann, G. and Cohen, E. (1996) Sociology and tourism, in Y. Apostopoloulos, S. Leivadi and A. Yiannakis (eds), *The Sociology of Tourism. Theoretical and Empirical Investigation.* London: Routledge. pp. 301–14.

Hayllard, B. and Griffin, T. (2005) The precinct experience: a phenomenological approach, *Tourism Management*, 26 (4): 517–28.

Jamal, T. and Hollinshead, K. (2001) Tourism and the forbidden zone: the underserved power of qualitative inquiry, *Tourism Management*, 22 (1): 63–82.

Lengkeek, J. (1996) On the multiple realities of leisure. A phenomenological approach to the otherness of leisure, *Society and Leisure*, 19: 23–40.

Lowenthal, D. (1961) Geography, experience and imagination. Towards a geographical epistemology, *Annals of the Association of American Geographers*, 51: 241–60.

Masberg, B. and Silverman, L. (1996) Visitor experiences at heritage sites – a phenomenological study, *Journal of Travel Research*, 34: 20–5.

Reichel, A., Fuchs, G. and Uriely, N. (2005) Israeli backpackers: The role of destination choice, *Annals of Tourism Research*, 36: 222–246.

Selby, M. (2004) *Understanding Urban Tourism Image, Culture and Experience.* London: IB Tauris.

key concepts in
tourism research

Selby, M., Selby, H. and Botterill, D. (2010) Tourism, image and fear of crime, in D. Botterill and T. Jones (eds), *Tourism and Crime: Key Concepts*. Oxford: Goodfellow Publishers. pp. 187–214.

Yiping Li (2000) Geographical consciousness and tourism experience, *Annals of Tourism Research*, 27 (4): 863–83.

Positivism

> **Definition** A research programme researching only the 'positive', namely, given, factual, sure and without any doubt and because of this it rejects metaphysics as theoretically impossible and practically without any use.

RELEVANCE

So what's all the fuss about when it comes to Positivism? It is hard to imagine what tourism research would look like today were it not for the key concept of Positivism and while it has almost become a term of derision in some circles this is no way to treat such an important influence in tourism research. Even if you are a firmly convinced 'interpretivist' there is still value in understanding what positivist science was trying to do and what caused it to ultimately fail. Many of you will, we are sure, still cling to the tenets of post-positivism in doing, and writing about, your research projects. For example, you will probably be encouraged to write yourself out of your research by adopting the 'third-person' form – 'the researcher found that' – you will assume that what you observe in your research is how the world 'is', you will present the 'facts' denying the value systems that underlie them, and no doubt you will justify your methods because they are universally 'scientific'. Oh, and if you use quantitative data and display frequency distributions in graphs and charts and perhaps use inferential statistics to identify correlations between variables, then that, too, has been inspired by Positivism. See what we mean …

APPLICATION

In academic tourism research positivism has held a significantly influential position, but has also experienced strong reactions against it over the recent past. Until the late 1990s, reviews of tourism research methods have concentrated on studies underpinned by positivist science, or assessments of quantitative methods and analyses (Riley and Love, 2000). The mood around this time was captured in a symposium held in 1996, 'Paradigms in Tourism Research', in Jyväskylä, Finland, which proved to be important in the development of tourism research. The intention of this symposium was 'to discuss the master paradigms influencing research, the various methods by which knowledge is accumulated and to promote dialog that encourages alternative approaches to the study of this field' (Riley and Love, 2000: 164). The feeling of resistance was well expressed by one conference reviewer: 'far too many conferences seem to be little more than mega-events given over to hundreds of papers that are merely recitals of official statistics or survey data' (Dann, 1996: 1).

At this juncture a quantitative versus qualitative debate (Walle 1997; Decrop, 1999) became more prominent in tourism research. Given the dominance of positivism as normative practice, we defer from making selections from the research literature of the time. Rather we suggest reading the entries in this book for Empiricism, Deduction, Modelling and Survey for examples of the ongoing legacy of positivism in tourism research.

In its initial stages, qualitative research has often been criticised for ignoring the tenets of 'good science'. Good science at that time was dictated by positivism as the prevailing paradigm. Qualitative researchers initially tried to meet these 'tenets' by refining the positivist concepts of corroboration and validation (Decrop 1999), for example through triangulation (Denzin and Lincoln, 1994). However, gradually the resistance against the suffocating demands of positivistism and quantitative methodology grew in importance. Grounded Theory was a predecessor, although it still harboured positivist influences. Subsequently, more qualitative 'paradigms' entered the tourism academy.

HISTORICAL DEVELOPMENT

The origins of the formation of science emerged most vigorously after its conflict with the dominant theistic philosophy of the Middle Ages.

The so-called birth of the new sciences in the 17th century provided a strong impetus. A clear example of the conflict and its resolution in favour of science was the collision between the assumptions of helio-centrism (represented by the Italian philosopher and astronomer Galileo) and those of the church. Gradually an intellectual community came into existence, believing in science and not in religious dogmatism, in tolerance and peace, and extolling a sense of being at one with nature. Subsequentially, the French philosopher Rene Descartes, the British empiricists (see Empiricism), other proponents in the philosophy of the Enlightenment and David Hume, all continued to develop a scientific way of thinking.

For many in the social scientific community, Auguste Comte (2009 [1844]) is assumed to be the father of Positivism. He claimed that history has shown that the arrival of scientific knowledge has occurred through three stages; religion, metaphysics and positivism. In the positivist stage the four characteristics described below by Kolakowski became integrated in a specific scientific approach. Comte also developed a sociology oriented towards achieving a more rational design of society, based on knowledge about the positive facts of social reality.

Kolakowski wrote a history of Positivism in his much quoted *Die Philosophie des Positivismus* (trans, 1972). His analysis centred around the development of four main streams of thought, or characteristics, that came to dominate the scientific field:

1 phenomenalism – there is no distinction in reality between essence and appearance;
2 nominalism – generalisations or abstractions are mere constructions;
3 value judgements – normative statements do not contain any core of knowledge;
4 the image of a unified science with a unified methodology.

After Comte's death in 1857, Positivism started its triumphal procession across the sciences with the main milestones being: Darwin's evolutionary theory; Bernard's discoveries in physiology and his focus on experimental rigidity that became the watchword for any scientist; as well as the utilitarianism of J.S. Mill. In the 20th century, the most inspiring period for Positivism started during the 1920s with the Wiener Kreis and its *Wissenschaftliche Weltauffassung*, the movement of logical positivism. The scientists and philosophers of the Vienna Circle took the view that if a phenomenon could not be verified, then it was untrue and did not exist. The corollary, of course, being that what has been proven after serious empirical testing is true and cannot be doubted. Everything else is in the realm of metaphysics and has no meaning at all.

During the 1920s and the 1930s of the last century this belief contained a powerful critique undercutting the influence of religion, other sources of 'irrational' ideas and the ideological misuse of science. Attacks on the emergent racist theories in Nazism and its subsequent rise in Central Europe forced a break-up of the Vienna circle as many of its proponents emigrated to the UK and the USA. Of course this also spread the influence of logical positivism and some of its basic principles influenced the linguistic and analytical tradition that became a crucial part of the Anglo-Saxon philosophy. For many in the social and human sciences since the 1960s, positivism lost its attraction. Logical positivists themselves recognised the problems of some of their positions and strove hard to find solutions but, ultimately accepted failure.

Post-positivism (Zammito, 2004) recognises these prevailing criticisms against logical positivism. It does not lead, however, to a rejection of Positivism outright and the ideal of one, unified science, but rather favours its reformation to meet these criticisms. It holds onto some of the basic assumptions of positivism: ontological realism, the possibility and desirability of objective truth, and the use of experimental methodology.

DESCRIPTION

In accordance with the idea of a unified science (Carnap, 1967) and later with critical rationalism (Popper, 2003), social science developed a positivistic methodology, based upon the success of the natural sciences. Hypotheses should be derived from scientific theories, its concepts operationalised through clearly defined variables, and tested by confirming (Carnap) or falsifying (Popper) hypotheses. The conclusions are related again to the theories that form the framework of hypotheses.

This methodology constitutes the basis of social scientific empirical research, taken from the legacy of Positivism. In social science when the relationship between theory and empirical testing is unclear, the argument states that being loyal to the scientific methodology will improve the relationship and develop more comprehensive theory. Through this positivist influence, education in methodology and its empirical testing continues to constitute a core element of the training of social scientists.

POTENTIAL CRITICISM

Positivism has been attacked from many perspectives including falsification, interpretivism and critical realism. First, a criticism shared with the natural sciences comes from Popper's falsification thesis. This position continues to shape post-positivist social science particularly in psychology and economics. Under falsification there is no certainty or absolute truth in science (see the concept Deduction). Falsification is fundamentally different from positivism's adherence to verification through induction, because it rejects any certainty in science. It is a demarcation criterion that separates science from non-science, but non-science does exist and may even be true (without, of course, ever being sure about it).

Interpretivism attacked positivism on ontological grounds (see Hermeneutics and Phenomenology) insisting on the separation of natural and social phenomenon. Critical Realism has insisted on the possibilities of metaphyisics in social scientific explanation through its explication of a separation between the transitive and intransitive objects of science.

CROSS REFERENCES

Critical Realism, Deduction, Empiricism, Modelling, Survey.

FURTHER READING

Generic

Carnap, R. (1967) *The Logical Structure of the World. Pseudoproblems in Philosophy.* Berkeley, CA: University of California Press.

Comte, A. (2009 [1844]) *A General View of Positivism.* Cambridge: Cambridge University Press.

Denzin, N.K. and Lincoln, Y.S. (eds) (1994) *Handbook of Qualitative Research.* Thousand Oaks, CA: Sage.

Kolakowski, L. (1972) *Positivist Philosophy: From Hume to the Vienna Circle.* Harmondsworth: Penguin.

Kuhn, T. (1962) *The Structure of Scientific Revolution.* Chicago, IL: University of Chicago Press.

Popper, K.R. (2003) *Conjectures and Refutations: The Growth of Scientific Knowledge.* London: Routledge.

Zammito, J.H. (2004) *A Nice Derangement of Epistemes. Post-positivism in the Study of Science from Quine to Latour.* Chicago, IL: University of Chicago Press.

positivism

Tourism specific

Dann, G. (1996) Symposium on paradigms in tourism research. The Newsletter of the International Academy for the Study of Tourism. Jyväskilä, Finland: International Sociological Association.

Decrop, A. (1999) Triangulation in qualitative tourism research, *Tourism Management*, 20 (1): 157–61.

Riley, R.W. and Love, L.L. (2000) The state of qualitative tourism research, *Annals of Tourism Research*, 27 (1): 164–87.

Walle, A.H. (1997) Quantitative versus qualitative tourism research, *Annals of Tourism Research* 240 (3): 524–36.

Post-colonialism

> **Definition** In Post-colonialism all parties involved have gone through a phase of colonial relationships, awakened from its legacies and built up a new way of understanding the emergent, economic, political and cultural networks around them.

RELEVANCE

An understanding of Post-colonialism can be very useful in studies of tourism and heritage. The heritage attractions of many tourism destinations are likely, in some way, to be linked to a period of colonialism. There are plentiful opportunities to study how heritage is represented through tourism and Post-colonialism provides a key concept in understanding how the ownership and representation of heritage can be controversial. The migration of people, often forced by coercion or economic necessity, and their cultural influence on the identity of a place, ironically, now provides the cultural diversity that so many destinations seek to promote as a part of their destination image. In a further twist to the post-colonial landscape, travel back to the 'homeland' is the motivation of many tourists in what has been labelled 'diasporic tourism'.

APPLICATION

The claims of a post-colonial era impact upon many areas of social and economic life. This is especially so in the case of tourism, which is *sui generis* closely related to global and local relationships between Western guests and non-Western hosts. Hall and Tucker (2004) provide the most comprehensive account of the links between tourism, colonialism and Post-colonialism. The chapters of their book demonstrate that post-colonial thinking poses many challenges and new lines of analysis in tourism research. The intricacies of global tourism involve power relationships in various degrees of subtlety. For example, in community based tourism, this new order leads to questions about local forms of community life, from the perspectives of 'local' cultures and in confrontation with the other relevant perspectives, in order to contribute to a relocation of the predominant Western perspective in the field. However, this is not straightforward and the subtlety of power is demonstrated in a study set in post-socialist Vietnam. Michaud and Turner (2006) investigated to what extent tourism dynamics today can be seen to be mirroring the French colonial scene of the past, suggesting similarities and distinctions between these two eras. Using 'representations' of tourism they show how multiple actors compete for control of tourism and identify 'economic victors' (Vietnamese and international tourists, local state authorities, Vietnamese and overseas entrepreneurs), and those largely left behind, namely, the ethnic minorities.

However, it is in the topic of heritage tourism that we find most references to a post-colonial discourse. Among these references, the monograph by Winter (2007) stands apart as a careful dissection of the historical and contemporary conditions of culture, politics and development enveloping the heritage monument at Angkor. Another striking example, demonstrating the contested nature of heritage sites, examines slavery as a feature of visitor attractions in the Southern states of the USA, the UK and West Africa. In Dann and Seaton (2001) for example, the presented interpretations of these historic sites look to educate visitors by sharing stories of the legendary American 'Old South'. However, the 'story' seems to have some 'black holes', literally and figuratively. Brochures and other promotional material have been analysed, but the stories of the slaves themselves, both then and now is missing. Slave quarters are referred to as servant quarters or carriage houses, and attempts to restore the balance in the story line are usually made upon special demand. The fact that tourism appears to be a natural successor to the plantation system, instead of its polar opposite, is the book's clear conclusion.

In a postmodern context, the selective presentation of slavery heritage 'for purposes of visitor entertainment trivialises and compromises the very object of its portrayal' (Dann and Seaton, 2001: 18). From a post-colonial stance, it remains logical that 'community healing occurs by keeping alive dissonant issues', rather than 'letting them rest' or 'sweeping them under the carpet' (Dann and Seaton, 2001: 20–1). Black discourse itself should get a prominent place, 'but there are no examples in this collection to the reactions of those depicted (or more realistically their descendants) to the ways in which they have been portrayed. There is thus a certain *voicelessness* to the accounts' (2001: 24). Obviously, in this type of heritage site, many pasts are involved. The subject of memorialisation as a construction of the various communities and their pasts needs to be dealt with in a subtle dialogue, leading to a situation where there are no voiceless groups. All these contributors, therefore, present 'a plurality of voices, bodies, populations and histories coming from "elsewhere" to disrupt the Euro-American sense of where the "centre" lies' (Chambers and Curti, 1996: 222).

HISTORICAL DEVELOPMENT

Within the limits of the colonial encounter there were two types of colonisation.

1 A relatively simple-minded type with a focus on the physical conquest of territories, which was very violent.
2 A complex type with a commitment to the conquest and occupation of minds, selves and cultures. This type was pioneered by rationalists, modernists and liberals who spread the message of civilisation to the uncivilised world.

The second form introduced 'enduring hierarchies of subjects and knowledge – the coloniser and the colonised, the scientific and the superstitious, the developed and the developing' (Prakash, 1995: 3). In a reflection of this colonial condition, post-coloniality produces narratives and counter-narratives in which 'all parties involved are awakened from the frustrations and are building new ways of understanding' (Prakash, 1995: 3). In this new, post-colonial, epistemological space (Hall and du Gay, 1996) discourses and counter-discourses emerge beyond 'orientalism' (Saïd, 2003), a concept symbolising the projections of the colonial West on the rest of the world. Foucault's (1966, 1977) analysis of the alliance between power and knowledge has been extended to the (post)-colonial conditions of the modern, global village. Eminent writers in literary criticism who followed Saïd and Hall, such as Spivak (1987, 1999) and Bhabha (1994), have worked in this same emergent post-colonial discourse. A post-colonial 'episteme', as circumscribed by Hall and others makes sense, considering the often hidden, colonial influences in various forms of sociological, anthropological and philosophical thinking. Hall *cum suis* relates the resistance to these colonial influences in our globalising world with its varying networks to this new discursive field he calls 'post-colonialism'.

Bhabha (1994) states that the culture of Western modernity must be relocated from a post-colonial perspective. The pastoral tendency in cultural anthropology that presents non-Western cultures as irrational, close to nature and primitive, has been unmasked as the projection of the over-stressed and over-civilised Western world. In a post-colonial episteme, this tendency has been relocated by various post-colonial perspectives or voices. Spivak (1987), criticises the narcissism of the liberal-feminist investigator who gazes at the silenced Third World women without hearing them representing themselves. This all ends, according to Spivak with a solipsistic confirmation of the investigator's discursive privilege: 'Her question, in the light of those silent women, is about her *own* identity rather than theirs …' (1987: 137, original emphasis). In response, a huge (post-colonial) literature has emerged on the position of women from the Southern part of the world, written by themselves (Castells, 2000). In this literature, various perspectives in diverse circumstances demonstrate gender power relationships in different parts of the world.

The question therefore emerges how the legitimating narratives of cultural domination can be displaced to reveal a 'third space' (Bhabha, 1994). In this third space, there is a need for a theory of hybridity (Hollinshead, 2007), in which room will be made for new, emergent voices and the translation of social differences, going beyond the polarities of Self and Other, and East and West. In this pluri-cultural, global village, there is a need for the perspectives of many involved voices, instead of one perspective of the all-knowing megaphone of pseudo-specialists. The challenging issue is to evoke many voices in a systematic manner within the confines of a post-colonial order. In this laboratory of a third space, this 'in-between'-world, the differences in culture, theoretical background *inter alia* are discussed without any assumed or presupposed hierarchies.

DESCRIPTION

The post-colonial episteme presents a well reasoned argument against the attempts by the tourism academy to strive for a non-biased universality in its scientific results. In contrast, how to operate with biases is the starting point for post-colonial analysis. An interesting path to address this challenge is offered by Clifford (1988) as a polyphonic dialogue in which all biased positions are 'in dialogue' from within an egalitarian perspective.

POTENTIAL CRITICISM

Post-colonialism in its essence is a question of power relationships and these relationships are everywhere. Therefore, the question of power relationships will re-emerge 'beyond post-colonialism' and we will be left to ask, 'did post-colonialism actually say anything new?'.

CROSS REFERENCES

Constructionism, Narrative, Postmodernism.

FURTHER READING

Generic

Bhabha, H.K. (1994) *The Location of Culture*. London: Routledge.

Castells, M. (2000) *The Information Age: Economy, Society and Culture*, Vols I, II and III. Oxford: Blackwell Publishers.

Chambers, I. and Curti, L. (eds) (1996) *The Post-Colonial Question: Common Skies, Divided Horizons*. London: Routledge.

Clifford, J. (1988) *The Predicament of Culture*. Cambridge, MA: Harvard University Press.

Foucault, M. (1966) *Les mots et les choses*. Paris: Gallimard.

Foucault, M. (1977) *Surveiller et punir: naissance de la prison*. Paris: Gallimard.

Hall, S. and du Gay, P. (eds) (1996) *Questions of Cultural Identity*. London: Sage.

Hall, M. and Tucker, H. (eds) (2004) *Tourism and Post-colonialism: Contested Discourses, Identities and Representations*. London: Routledge.

Prakash, G. (1995) *After Colonialism: Imperial Histories and Post-colonial Displacements*. Princeton, NJ: Princeton University Press.

Saïd, E. (2003) *Orientalism*. London: Penguin Books.

Spivak, G. (1987) *In Other Worlds: Essays in Cultural Politics*. London: Methuen.

Spivak, G. (1999) *A Critique of Post-Colonial Reason*. Cambridge, MA: Harvard University Press.

Tourism specific

Dann, G.M.S. (2002) *The Tourist as a Metaphor of the Social World*. New York: CABI Publishing.

Dann, G.M.S. and Seaton, A.V. (eds) (2001) *Slavery, Contested Heritage and Thanatourism*. New York: The Haworth Press.

Hollinshead, K. (2007) Worldmaking and the transformation of culture: the enlargement of Meethan's analysis of tourism and global change, in I. Ateljevic, A. Pritchard and N. Morgan (eds), *The Critical Turn in Tourism Studies: Innovative Research Methods*. Amsterdam: Elsevier. pp. 165–93.

Michaud, J. and Turner, S. (2006) Contending visions of a hill-station in Vietnam, *Annals of Tourism Research*, 33 (3): 785–808.

Winter, T. (2007) *Post-Conflict Heritage, Post-colonial Tourism*. Abingdon: Routledge.

Postmodernism

> **Definition** A stream of thought that comes after (post)modernism, which implies either an intensified continuation (synonymous to 'late' or 'high' modernity) or a rejection and criticism of modern times and modernism.

RELEVANCE

If you are looking to dismantle orthodoxy in tourism studies through your research project, then there are few better places to start than here. Postmodernism has fuelled a process of re-examining the fixed categories of social life that have created the notion of tourism. Studies of cities as tourism destinations, a reversal of the normalised order of tourism wherein people 'escape' from the city for holidays, for example, illustrates the postmodern argument that the modern categories of life are breaking down. The city beach is just one example of this de-differentiation and for some commentators postmodernism speaks to the possible 'end of tourism'. While we would not go that far it is clear that tourism is a function of, rather than an escape from, society and as a commentary on changes in society, Postmodernism has much to offer in any analysis of contemporary tourism. If you choose to locate your research within Postmodernism there are consequences. The way in which postmodernists are playful about their analyses and their continuing quest to dismantle modernist sureties means that there are no particular ways of researching or conventions on how to report postmodernist research. You will need a very supportive supervisor for research projects that adopt this key concept.

APPLICATION

According to Urry (1990) contemporary Western tourists do not experience reality directly because they are constantly presented with pseudo-events. The images generated of different tourist 'gazes' constitute a 'closed self-perpetuating system of illusions which provide the tourist with the basis for selecting and evaluating potential places to visit' (1990: 7). John Urry has been the crucial theorist in translating the ideas of postmodernism into tourism studies. Against a background of post-Fordist consumption, the tourist is characterised by an increasing diversity of preference. The media plays a crucial role in the way in which tourist 'gazes' are constructed, added to this there is a proliferation of alternative sights and attractions determined by lifestyle choices of tourists. As a consequence, there is a rapid turnover of tourist sites and experiences linked to fast-moving changes in fashion coupled with 'de-differentiation' – a process of blurring distinctions – between the previously, fixed concepts of tourism, leisure, culture, retailing, education, sport and hobbies. Demarcation lines between these concepts seem to disappear, new words are invented such as 'edutainment' and just as previously, essentialist demarcations like authenticity or identity fall away. Under Postmodernism, recent research has challenged the validity of concepts such as identity and authenticity – tourists seem to know there is no authenticity, only games or texts being played, determined by preconceived gazes (Fawcett and Cormack, 2001; Herbert, 2001; Wang, 1999; Buchmann et al., 2010; Martin, 2010).

Postmodernist thinking has proved inspirational across many of the contexts of tourism research. For example, the diverse interpretations of built heritage as a part of tourism development in a developing country is demonstrated in Nuryanti's (1996) study of Indonesia. Other examples of the postmodern zeitgeist, in which heritage tourism is identified, presented, interpreted and contested by multiple stakeholders are Las Vegas and the Gold Coast (Weaver, 2010). In urban tourism the postmodern city has appeared in the literature (Hall, 2009). One such example considers the city of Manchester, a former industrial centre in the North West of England, that is portrayed as a 'Hollywood of the North' and Schofield (1996) provides an example of postmodern heritage tourism seen through cinematographic images of its past and present.

Urry's gaze has also been applied to the Santa Claus Industry in Finland (Pretes,1995) and to modern and postmodern theories in tourism (Urlely, 1997). Hip-hop music has been considered as a basic landmark in the tourism industry as a special form of 'gaze', a unique constructing of the 'other' (Xie et al., 2007). Through an emic perspective on postmodern theory, the originally fixed categories of Israeli backpackers to India were replaced by a complexity of tourist experiences, full of contradictions (Maoz and Bekerman, 2010).

Postmodernism has also influenced writings on methodology, dark tourism, tourism attraction systems, seaside tourism, sustainable tourism, marketing, cruise tourism and many other topics. A neglected part of the postmodern project in tourism research, however, has been to acknowledge the importance of feminist and critical theory on embodiment. Johnston's (2001) study of the particular tourist gaze created by the Sydney Gay and Lesbian Mardi Gras Parade is an exception. In order to subvert the masculinity of tourism discourse, this study offers an embodied account of a tourism hallmark event and results in a feminist discourse, supported by postmodern thought.

HISTORICAL DEVELOPMENT

At the end of the last century, conversation turned to an emergent, different type of society. This was in large part due to the developing age of information, coupled with the importance of transnational organisations, outweighing national and regional activities in economic and political importance. As a result of the enormous growth of consumption and 'free' choice of the consumer, everyday life seemed to become fragmented and complex. It was against this background that a new way of thinking came into existence (Vattimo, 1988; Harvey, 1990).

Already in the 1950s American poets, such as Charles Olson, accused modernism of haughtiness. Olson stated that instead of this attitude one should humbly accept reality in all its facets, as spontaneously as possible. Spontaneity also dominated in the Beat-generation which reacted against the rationalism of the 1950s. During the 1960s there was an outburst of protest inspired by explorations of sexuality, spontaneity, irrationality and mysticism, set alongside a resistance against the establishment, which came together in a counter-culture represented by hippies living at the margins of post-industrial society. Classical categories like serious high art versus mass art, artist versus public, professional versus layman, were abolished as being repressive borderlines. Everything was permitted in art as in other areas of everyday life. Value hierarchies were considered as elitist and repressive. Literature was not about reality anymore, but instead there were only constructions or models that produce reality. Eclecticism entered the argument, because these constructions were relative and not related to an absolute reality anymore. This relativism was very much related to what postmodern philosophy (Lyotard, 1984) called the end of the meta-narratives.

Meta-narratives, the big stories that had enchanted Western civilisation, were in decay. People did not live under the spell of Christianity, Marxism or the modernist belief in rational progress anymore. Postmodernists constructed their own life stories. If language is power, then the power position of a discourse can be undermined and new discourses (realities) can be installed. Various groups of mainly marginalised people claimed their own discourses. Feminism, for example, embraced a postmodernist approach and plurality replaced the sureties of the past. As a consequence in the metropolis, the centres of postmodern life, citizens moved eclectically between various stories which occurred simultaneously. In fashion, in music or in youth culture, various vogues made their way to the public simultaneously. In the classroom up until the 1980s teachers were confronted with either hippies or (later) punk rockers, but since then they saw neo-punks sitting next to Goths and careerists in the same classroom. In art, a new commercial form of Postmodernism developed apart from avant-gardists. In video-clips or in films such as *Dive*, ordinary stories were combined with beautiful, artistic images without any significant meaning. Postmodernism set the agenda for many social-scientific debates. The post modern city has been described as a fun-city, in which art and culture were considered as tourist attractions in city marketing and where lifestyles replaced the taste preferences based on classes. Multiple identities have been constructed in interacting, pluralist communities all over the globe and the 'higher arts' are in the grip of commercialisation and a marketing-approach.

DESCRIPTION

Feyerabend (1975) introduced the concept of 'anything goes' into the philosophy of science and this concept seems to dominate postmodern social science. Its most fervent supporters demonstrate their enthusiasm in response to the so-called 'crisis of representation' that has opened the door to qualitative, interpretive research. In strong constructionist approaches, the relationship between theory and reality has been reversed, inspired by postmodern thinking. Discourses shape the formation of theory and this, combined with power relations, produces reality. If we accept this argument, then the importance of the relationship between (critical) discourse analysis and postmodernity becomes clearer. Discourses and counter-discourses emerge within power constellations and need to be deciphered through critical discourse analysis.

POTENTIAL CRITICISM

The strongest criticism of postmodernist thought focuses on the total absence of reality as an important concept. How do postmodernists avoid the relativist trap? If all discourses are accepted, by what criteria can Postmodernism claim any superiority? How can the material conditions of the starving and homeless be improved? What universal human rights exist? How might social progress be achieved? Critics of Postmodernism argue that if human beings cannot bridge their differences and find shared values then the emancipatory, democratic project embraced by many postmodern social theorists will never be realised.

CROSS REFERENCES

Constructionism, Document Analysis, Epistemology.

FURTHER READING

Generic

Feyerabend, P. (1975) *Against Method*. London: Humanities Press.
Harvey, D. (1990) *The Condition of Postmodernity*. Oxford: Blackwell.
Lyotard, J. (1984) *The Postmodern Condition*. Manchester: Manchester University Press.
Vattimo, G. (1988) *The End of Modernity*. Oxford: Polity Press.

Tourism specific

Buchmann, A., Moore, K. and Fisher, D. (2010) Experiencing film tourism: authenticity & fellowship, *Annals of Tourism Research*, 37 (1): 229–48.
Fawcett, C. and Cormack, P. (2001) Guarding authenticity at literary tourism sites, *Annals of Tourism Research*, 28 (3): 686–704.
Hall, T. (2009) Urban tourism, in R. Kitchin and N. Thrift (eds), *International Encyclopedia of Human Geography*. Oxford: Elsevier.

Herbert, D. (2001) Literary places, tourism and the heritage experience, *Annals of Tourism Research*, 28 (2): 312–33.

Johnston, L. (2001) (Other) bodies and tourism studies, *Annals of Tourism Research*, 28 (1): 180–201.

Maoz, D. and Bekerman, Z. (2010) Searching for Jewish answers in Indian resorts: the postmodern traveller, *Annals of Tourism Research*, 37 (2): 423–39.

Martin, K. (2010) Living pasts: contested tourism authenticities, *Annals of Tourism Research*, 37 (2): 537–54.

Nuryanti, W. (1996) Heritage and postmodern tourism, *Annals of Tourism Research*, 23 (2): 249–60.

Pretes, M. (1995) Postmodern tourism: the Santa Claus industry, *Annals of Tourism Research*, 22 (1): 1–15.

Schofield, P. (1996) Cinematographic images of a city: alternative heritage tourism in Manchester, *Tourism Management*, 17 (5): 333–40.

Urlely, N. (1997) Theories of modern and postmodern tourism, *Annals of Tourism Research*, 24 (4): 982–85.

Urry, J. (1990) *The Tourist Gaze: Leisure and Travel in Contemporary Societies*. London: Sage.

Wang, N. (1999) Rethinking authenticity in tourism experience, *Annals of Tourism Research*, 26 (2): 349–70.

Weaver, D. (2010) Contemporary tourism: heritage as heritage tourism: evidence from Las Vegas and Gold Coast, *Annals of Tourism Research*, 38 (1): 249–67.

Xie, P., Osumare, H. and Ibrahim, A. (2007) Gazing the hood: hip-hop as tourism attraction, *Tourism Management*, 28 (2): 452–60.

·········· Realism ··········

> **Definition** 'Realists assert the actual, or possible, existence of some disputed entity, which may be a sub-atomic particle, a social structure, or the world or universe itself' (Outhwaite, 2004: 929).

RELEVANCE

Realism offers the prospect of tourism research that combines creative imagination with the possibility of scientific explanation. Students of tourism that are looking to insert some 'depth' into their research projects by: going beyond the surface of events and experiences, seeking to unify the natural and the social in tourism research, and wishing to retain the aspiration of an explanatory social science for tourism will find an exploration of the key concept of Realism invaluable.

APPLICATION

The self-identification of tourism research that is realist, in the sense of a scientific depth realism, is relatively uncommon. However, the tendency in research publications to present conceptual models of aspects of tourism (see Modelling) and the relative prioritisation of induction over deduction (see Deduction) in concept and theory building would seem to mirror a realist aspiration, without explicitly acknowledging the debates about Realism in the social sciences. Evidence of those debates is most strong in a small but growing body of work in tourism from those authors who have explored two distinctive neo-realist 'camps', actor-network theory and Critical Realism.

Actor-network theory or ANT, the acronym by which it has become better known, often with the prefix 'after' as in after-ANT, is now appearing in a number of studies of tourism. The realist insistence of ANT upon materialities and the 'stuff' of the world is nicely demonstrated by van der Duim (2007) in his seminal article on Tourismscapes. This sensibility within ANT, that nothing is simply 'social', combined with an obsession for the 'mess of material practices' directs Duim (2007) to consider the role of both human and, controversially, non-human actors in tourism development and sustainability. Consequentially, in his published doctoral thesis he demonstrates in a series of case studies how material practices as well as human agents have powers to shape the social world of tourism as we know it.

A second example by Ren et al. (2010) illuminates the attention in ANT given to 'relationality' and to 'processes and practices' in their study entitled 'Constructing tourism research: a critical enquiry'. In what is otherwise a helpful explication of ANT to tourism research, the use of the word 'constructing' with its referent to social Constructionism is rather unfortunate. While the attendance to relationality – the post-structuralist insistence that nothing, including tourism research, exists in and of itself – and to process – the idea that it is the practicing and interacting that gives tourism research the shape and continuities that it has – ANT should not be misconstrued as social Constructionism. As John Law, a major figure in ANT has recently commented:

realism

... if ANT is realist (and I propose, of course controversially, that it is) then it obviously isn't a form of critical realism ... Whatever else it is, 'after ANT' is *not* socially constructivist. It *doesn't* say that realities are constructed by people or interest groups. The argument it makes is quite different. (Law, 2009: 70–1, original emphasis)

Critical Realist scholarship in tourism has already been dealt with in its own section in this book and readers are referred there for a refresher. However, the invitation by Ren et al. (2010) to explore the messy post-structuralist world of contingent social relations and material practices in tourism research is also the starting point for Botterill (2007) in his critical realist attack on the rise of the 'situated voice' in tourism research. The argument he develops exposes at least one of the differences between the critical realist and the after-ANT 'camps' of realism that underlies the assertion in Law's quote above. The possibility of theorising the social world is strongly resisted in after-ANT circles but for critical realists the scientific project in the social sciences is still very much alive, albeit in a re-constructed form.

HISTORICAL DEVELOPMENT

Realism as a movement in Western intellectual life is, first, a movement of the humanities in the mid-19th century and, second, a response to mid-20th-century scholarship on the history of science, in particular the work of Thomas Kuhn. The painting of the French artist Courbet, in particular, *A Burial at Ornans* and *The Studio of the Painter* are classic examples of the realist art movement that simultaneously sought to challenge the idealism of art in the 'salon' and to depict the material conditions of life, class and power in mid-19th-century France. The realism movement also developed its own protagonists in literature.

Kuhn's thesis (first published in 1962 in German and in 1972 translated into English) on science as a social practice informed by philosophical transformations – shaping and being shaped by the societies that made it possible – inspired an array of potential routes for social science. In sociology, for example, here was the perfect ground for relativist and constructionist debunking of the authority of the scientific project, best expressed perhaps by Peter Winch in his essay that challenged the very idea of a social science. For others it fuelled scepticism against the prospects of a unity of method in the social and natural sciences and reinforced an ontological divide between the social and natural worlds. The turn to interpretivism within the social sciences and its incumbent limited aspiration for social science, to speak only of the interpretation of meaning in subject to subject exchange, led to the formulation of a divisive qualitative versus quantitative argument.

But to limit the social science project in this way was not enough for the early thinkers on depth scientific realism. First, Rom Harré then Russell Keat and John Urry, Ted Benton and Roy Bhaskar sought to argue for the possibility of an explanatory social science that would 'aspire to the standards of empirical and theoretical rigour of the natural sciences, while fully acknowledging the indispensably communicative-interpretive dimensions of social life' (Benton, 2009: 211). In doing so it would also, just as Courbet's paintings had done more than a century before, open the possibility of alternative understandings of the conditions and constraints that challenged representations of 'common sense'.

DESCRIPTION

Realist approaches embrace the creative imagination in transcending observations of social life in order to provide accounts of reality. As we have shown above in our discussion of its application in tourism research the limits of the outcomes of a realist social science are disputed. However, for most researchers drawn to scientific realism it is the possibility of combining creative imagination, metaphor and models to understand the underlying entities, relations and mechanisms that explain observed patterns that recaptures the potential of a science of the social world.

POTENTIAL CRITICISM

Disputes still rage on in respect to the claim of depth scientific realism to close the ontological divide between the natural and social. Critique of realism at the meta-level is difficult to distil into a few sentences but at its heart are the competing pre-paradigmatic claims of the social constructionist and post-structuralist positions on the possibility of a social science.

CROSS REFERENCES

Critical Realism, Critical Theory, Deduction, Figurationalism.

Generic

Benton, T. (2009) Conclusion: philosophy, materialism and nature – comments and reflections, in S. Moog and R. Stones (eds) *Nature, Social Relations and Human Needs: Essays in Honour of Ted Benton*. Basingstoke: Palgrave Macmillan. pp. 208–43.

Law, J. (2009) Practicing nature and culture: an essay for Ted Benton, in S. Moog and R. Stones (eds) *Nature, Social Relations and Human Needs: Essays in Honour of Ted Benton*. Basingstoke: Palgrave Macmillan. pp. 208–43.

Outhwaite, W. (2004) Realism, in M. Lewis-Beck, R. Bryman and T.F. Liao (eds), *The SAGE Encyclopaedia of Social Science Research Methods*. Thousand Oaks, CA: Sage. p. 929.

Tourism specific

Botterill, D. (2007) A realist critique of the situated voice in tourism studies, in I. Ateljevic, N. Morgan and A. Pritchard (eds) *The Critical Turn in Tourism Studies: Innovative Research Methodologies*. Oxford: Elsevier. pp. 121–30.

Duim, R. van der (2007) 'Tourismscapes' an actor-network perspective, *Annals of Tourism Research*, 34 (4): 961–76.

Ren, C., Pritchard, A. and Morgan, N. (2010) Constructing tourism research: a critical inquiry, *Annals of Tourism Research*, 37 (4): 885–904.

key concepts in
tourism research

Repertory Grid

Definition The Repertory Grid is a research tool for capturing the ways in which an external reality is constructed by an individual.

RELEVANCE

If you are looking for a way of working in your research project that captures personal accounts of tourism experiences, then exploring what the Repertory Grid has to offer should prove valuable. The gains that can be made by having a sophisticated means to capturing the meaning of experiences can also be combined with survey work to enable a larger sample of respondents.

APPLICATION

The Repertory Grid was a popular technique in studies of the environment, for example in architecture and studies of environmental perception, in the 1970s. An early citation of the technique in the tourism literature was by Stringer (1984) in the *Annals of Tourism Research*. Human geographers adopted the technique to explore perceptions of holiday destinations and the Repertory Grid became popular in both generic and tourism-specific marketing research. In these studies, the elements were often countries or specific destination regions of countries. In parallel with Kelly's original use of the Repertory Grid as facilitative of personal change, researchers have applied the technique to measure changes in perceptions of destinations and 'self' as a result of a holiday (Botterill, 1989; Botterill and Crompton, 1996). More recently the Repertory Grid has been used in studies of historic sites (Naoi et al., 2006), destination image (Coshall, 2000; Pike, 2002, 2007; McNicol, 2004), museums and galleries (Caldwell and Coshall, 2003), nature tourism (Waitt et al., 2003) and urban tourism (Selby, 2004).

HISTORICAL DEVELOPMENT

The Repertory Grid was developed by George Alexander Kelly in his therapeutic practice in the USA. He wanted to be able to enter the personal world of his clients and saw the Repertory Grid as a way of displaying significant aspects of his clients' world, for example their relationships, prior to making therapeutic interventions. The Repertory Grid was, therefore, designed to facilitate personal change. The grid he used specified elements that were role labels for significant people in his clients' worlds, these included: mother, father, a friend I admire, a family member I dislike, and so on. In this way the client was able to insert the names of his or her own social circle but the process retained some structure that would be shared – we all are likely to have individuals in our lives playing the roles in Kelly's elements. Later in his work, Kelly published a *Theory of Personal Constructs* that attempted to provide a constructivist account of human behaviour. Kelly was strongly influenced by Phenomenology and by Social Constructionism. He wanted to provide a more liberating account of the human condition than that provided by the determinism of psycho-analysis and behaviourism. Personal Construct Psychology, as it has become known, is the result of the work of many other psychologists who have further developed

Kelly's original ideas. It continues to be used in psycho-therapeutic settings, particularly counselling.

DESCRIPTION

There are three components to a Repertory Grid. On the horizontal axis are a set of 'Elements', these can be provided by the researcher or by the respondent and are representative of what is to be construed. 'Constructs' form the vertical axis of the grid. These are always bi-polar and may be provided by the researcher but are more likely elicited from the respondent. In the main body of the grid the respondent records evaluations of each element against each construct. Often this is a numerical score and allows the application of multivariate statistical analysis.

The Repertory Grid requires a respondent and a researcher to engage in a process called construct elicitation. Kelly devised a technique that he called 'triading'. The respondent would be presented with three cards each with the name of a person in the set of elements. The question is put to the respondent, 'In what way are any two of these people similar and yet different from the third?' The descriptor word or phrase of the similarity between two elements would be recorded as one pole of a construct, the difference descriptor would become the negative pole. The construct descriptors are not necessarily logical opposites but they are meaningful contrasting descriptions of the client's world. In this way the derived data could be said to be ideographic. This question is repeated using different triads of elements until no new constructs emerged. The significant people in a client's life (elements) might then be ranked against the constructs in order to show how they are perceived by the respondent. Elements labelled 'self' and 'perfect self' were added by Kelly to sharpen the relationship between the client and his family and acquaintances. Kelly also developed a way of moving 'up' and 'down' a client's Personal Constructs, he called this Laddering. In an article arising from his doctoral research, Martin Selby demonstrates how the Repertory Grid can be used in tourism research. Selby (2004) conducted informal semi-structured interviews with tourists in three cities incorporating a conversational form of construct elicitation. He subsequently compiled a large grid of personal constructs derived from these conversations that he subsequently reduced to capture generic, yet salient, constructs for urban tourism.

The techniques have been further refined by researches from the Personal Construct Psychology community in order to apply the Repertory

Grid and Personal Construct Psychology to a broader range of subjects. Some researchers have used construct elicitation in a softer more conversational form while others have developed techniques to provide narrative analysis. There are a number of very useful guides to using the Repertory Grid (Fransella et al., 2004; Fromm, 2004; Jankowicz, 2004).

POTENTIAL CRITICISM

The majority of criticisms of the Repertory Grid emerge from those opposed to mechanistic and scientific accounts of human behaviour. Although the Repertory Grid produces meaningful, ideographic data that prioritises the respondent's views and humanises the research process, for some critics the ontology of bi-polar and hierarchical constructs that sits behind Kelly's approach is still too linear and scientific. The scoring of elements against the constructs and the subsequent application of multivariate statistics adds weight to these criticisms. The difficult challenge for researchers, that the Repertory Grid partially addresses, is how data that is meaningful to individuals can be aggregated into a research tool that can be applied to larger numbers of respondents. The use of element labels that are consistent across the construct elicitation process provides one part of a solution, as is the collapsing of personal constructs into a smaller number of frequently occurring constructs as shown in the example of Selby's study below. For some researchers, however, such an approach is regarded as too reductionist.

CROSS REFERENCES

Constructionism, Phenomenology.

FURTHER READING

Generic

Fransella, F., Bell, R. and Bannister, D. (2004) *A Manual for Repertory Grid Technique*, 2nd edn. Chichester: Wiley.
Fromm, Martin. (2004) *Introduction to the Repertory Grid Interview*. Münster: Waxmann.
Jankowicz, D. (2004) *The Easy Guide to Repertory Grids*. Chichester: Wiley.

Tourism specific

Botterill, T.D. (1989) Humanistic tourism? Personal constructs of a tourist: Sam visits Japan. *Leisure Studies*, 8 (3): 281–93.

Botterill, T.D. and Crompton, J.L. (1996) Two case studies exploring the nature of tourist's experience, *Journal of Leisure Research*, 28 (1): 57–82.

Caldwell, N. and Coshall, J. (2003) Tourists' preference structures for London's Tate Modern gallery: the implications for strategic marketing, *Journal of Travel & Tourism Marketing*, 14 (2): 23–45.

Coshall, J.T. (2000) Measurement of tourists' images: the repertory grid approach, *Journal of Travel Research*, 39 (1): 85–9.

McNicol, B.J. (2004) Group destination images of proposed tourism resort developments: identifying resident versus developer contrasts, *Tourism Analysis*, 9 (1/2): 41–53.

Naoi, T., Airey, D., Iijima, S. and Niininen, O. (2006) Visitors' evaluation of an historical district: Repertory Grid Analysis and Laddering Analysis with photographs, *Tourism Management*, 27 (3): 420–36.

Pike, S. (2002) The use of repertory grid analysis to elicit salient short-break holiday destination attributes in New Zealand, *Journal of Travel Research*, 41 (3): 315–19.

Pike, S. (2007) Current issues in method and practice repertory grid analysis in group settings to elicit salient destination image attributes, *Current Issues in Tourism*, 10 (4): 378–92.

Selby, M. (2004) Consuming the city: conceptualizing and researching urban tourist knowledge, *Tourism Geographies*, 6 (2): 186–207.

Stringer, P. (1984) Studies in the socio-environmental psychology of tourism, *Annals of Tourism Research*, 11: 147–66.

Waitt, G., Lane, R. and Head, L. (2003) The boundaries of nature tourism, *Annals of Tourism Research*, 30 (3): 523–45.

·· Survey ··

Definition Social surveys collect data in a standardised way from a sample of respondents enabling the data to be codified and analysed.

RELEVANCE

An old favourite of tourism researchers and still of great value if you are wanting to collect descriptive data about tourism activity. Recent web-based applications in digital format provide a new solution to administering a survey to more mobile populations than the tried and tested postal, telephone and face-to-face formats. Remember, investing time in survey design, question formulation and testing, and sampling protocols results in better quality social surveys. If you get these right then collecting and analysing the data is very much easier.

APPLICATION

Social surveys continue to be an important research tool for tourism researchers. While it might appear to be something of an overstatement some 40 years on, such was its dominance that there were times in the early 1970s when the majority of tourism research seemed simply to equate to yet another social survey. As we have demonstrated in this book, the situation has changed dramatically and contemporary tourism researchers now apply a plethora of methods in their studies, however we would still argue that the social survey is an important concept in tourism research, particularly to governments and industry. Critics of its early dominance in tourism research have pointed out that the facts derived from surveys became, erroneously, the 'truth' about tourism, a positivist irony.

Despite the reservations of some university-based researchers, governments and tourism businesses continue to depend on the survey method for the collection of statistics about tourism. Longitudinal studies at a country's points of entry and departure are used to monitor international tourism flows. Household surveys gather data on a range of social trends including holiday taking. These data are often used to provide market intelligence to the tourism industry (see, for example, Barber, 2009). A separate industry of consumer behaviour and market research companies has been built around the social survey and it has become an accepted facet of social life in many nations.

Such is the ubiquitous nature of the social survey it is indeed a daunting task to attempt to summarise its application to tourism research. Recent examples are provided here to demonstrate the currency of the survey method. Surveys of tourists (Haukeland et al., 2010), hosts (Ryan and Aicken, 2010) and employees (Robinson and Beesley, 2010) abound, and more recently tourism students and faculty have been pulled into the social survey net (Sanders and Armstrong, 2010). Social surveys are conducted using a range of data gathering processes. Face-to-face, post, and telephone surveys continue to provide the most robust applications of a method that depends on a rigorous process of survey instrument development and a formulaic application of statistical sampling.

Social surveys presume a relatively static population with fixed characteristics such as permanent addresses, used in sampling, and land-line telephones used in interviewing. Trends in mobile lifestyles and innovations in personal communications technology, however, are challenging the designers of social surveys to maintain its effectiveness as a reliable data gathering tool. In response, the social survey is making its presence felt in electronic form and versions of web-based survey software now facilitate the tracking of more mobile populations.

HISTORICAL DEVELOPMENT

Commentators generally agree that the social survey owes its origins to the work of Victorian reformers who sought to document the conditions of the poor during industrialisation in the 19th century. Documenting the patterns of unemployment, poverty, health and consumption became particularly important to governments during the Great Depression of the 1930s and in the ensuing Second World War in order to devise policy interventions aimed at alleviating hardship. In the USA, the research units of the military recruited a number of young scholars who more latterly became the founders of the modern social survey (for example, Merton, Lazersfeld, Likert and Gutman). After 1945, these scholars helped to establish centres of survey research excellence in the university sector and contributed to the development of the market research and political research industries.

The technique of the social survey was developing at a time when the social sciences took a distinctly quantitative turn aided by developments in computing. Surveys proved immensely popular because they provided data in standardised and numerical form fuelling the explorations of computer power in analysing large data sets. The social survey became closely associated with Positivism in the social sciences, although the implied unity of philosophical position and method was assumed through convergence in practice rather than forged in a tightly argued intellectual sense. The rejection of Positivism does not seem to have weakened the credibility given to the social survey although it is more common nowadays to see the survey used as a part of a mixed method research strategy. The social survey can be deployed in tourism research by both realists and social constructionists but, of course, with differing presumptions and rationales for its adoption.

DESCRIPTION

There are excellent guidebooks to social survey design and use available (see, for example, Fowler, 2009). The survey's major strength is its ability to capture a large amount of information from many people simultaneously. Surveys might appear to be a fairly straightforward and simple means of collecting data. However, in order to meet rigorous standards of reliability (the extent to which questions measure the same thing over time and between respondents) and validity (the extent to which the survey measures what it intended to measure), considerable investment is put into developing the questions used and the sampling process. It is common to refine a survey instrument through trialling, often requiring many iterations. Surveys depend on three assumed behaviours of respondents, all of which may be corrupted. Respondents should read or hear the questions and interpret them as intended. They are also expected to reflect on their personal experiences before answering. Finally, the survey method expects honesty from the respondents.

POTENTIAL CRITICISM

Critics of surveys will point to the premises that allow their creation. As the social survey is without doubt a vehicle for gathering observable facts, then the critiques of Positivism in the social sciences also apply. The presumption that social phenomenon can be reduced to discrete and measurable variables, without losing something of their meaning, is fundamentally flawed, some will argue. Weaker variants of this line of criticism will focus on the choice of variables, and the measures adopted, to attack the reliability and validity of the data. Others will point to the persistent problem of non-response rate as undermining the confidence of social survey findings.

The alleged value-free quality of social surveys has also come under attack. Even when not explicitly declared by the researcher, the choice of topics and the formulation of questions in a questionnaire are derived from a certain theoretical position. Feminist researchers have long argued that patriarchal process is reinforced by the masculinist predetermination of the object under investigation and in some circles still reject the social survey as a legitimate research tool for this reason (see Feminism).

CROSS REFERENCES

Empiricism, Modelling, Positivism.

Generic

Fowler, F.J. Jr (2009) *Survey Research Methods*, 4th edn. London: Sage.

Tourism specific

Barber, S. (2009) Britain's coaches: partnership and passengers, *Tourism Insights*, March, unpaginated.

Haukeland, J.V., Grue, B., Veisten, K., Fredman, P. and Tyrväinen, L. (2010) Turning national parks into tourist attractions: nature orientation and quest for facilities, *Scandinavian Journal of Hospitality and Tourism*, 10 (3): 248–71.

Robinson, R.N.S. and Beesley, L.G. (2010) Linkages between creativity and intention to quit: an occupational study of chefs, *Tourism Management*, 31 (6): 765–76.

Ryan, C. and Aicken, M. (2010) The destination image gap – visitors' and residents' perceptions of place: evidence from Waiheke Island, New Zealand, *Current Issues in Tourism*, 13 (6): 541–61.

Sanders, D. and Armstrong, E.K. (2010) Understanding students' perceptions and experience of a tourism management field trip: the need for a graduated approach, *Journal of Hospitality & Tourism Education*, 20 (4): 29–37.

key concepts in
tourism research

····· Symbolic Interactionism ·····

Definition A school of social scientific thought that foregrounds the co-acting ('joint action', Blumer [1969]) behaviour of people whose actions can only be understood within a continuous practice of interpretation and reinterpretation during social interaction.

174

RELEVANCE

If you are hoping to investigate a small group of like-minded tourists, what we might call a subculture, then this key concept has much to offer. Take, for example, adventure tourists on a trek or volunteer tourists working on a conservation project, then Symbolic Interactionism offers you a way in which you might better capture the social meaning attributed by these participants to their chosen activity. The idea of 'sensitising concepts' is a very useful way of preparing yourself for the kind of participant observation fieldwork favoured by researchers from this tradition, because it provides some markers or pointers against which to organise your observations.

APPLICATION

Symbolic Interactionism was brought to the attention of tourism researchers in the late 1980s via a series of articles published in the *Annals of Tourism Research* (Colton, 1987, 1988; Brown, 1988). These authors introduced the basic tenets of Symbolic Interactionism; humans as sense-making beings, the construction of meaning and self identity and sensitising concepts. In an article first published in 1954, Herbert Blumer counterpoints the sensitising concepts of Social Interactionism with the definitive concepts he finds in social theory development through hypothesis testing and operational definition. Sensitising concepts provide the researcher with a general sense of guidance in approaching the field, as he puts it, 'definitive concepts provide prescriptions of what to see, sensitising concepts merely suggest the direction along which to look' (Blumer, 1954: 6).

We can get a feel for sensitising concepts from a number of articles in the tourism literature. For example, Honggen Xiao (1997) tests the homogeneity of social life in two nearby cities in China by studying the interactions between tourists and residents. In the Haug et al. (2007) study of Norwegian seasonal migrants to Spain the concepts of novelty and strangeness (after Simmel) suggest the kind of a guidance that Blumer imagines sensitised concepts provide in the field. Ryan and Gu (2010) show how complex symbolic values of different (Western and Buddhist) perspectives are enmeshed in tourism experiences in their study of the 4th Buddhist festival in Wutaishan, China. The legacy of Symbolic Interactionism in their study is made clear in the conclusion when they say, 'It concludes that the festival exists as a multi-layered event involving economics, politics, faith, entertainment and prestige – each of which creates its own set of interpretations contextualised in the evolving state of Chinese tourism' (Ryan and Gu, 2010: 167). However, the symbolic interactionist project has not convinced everyone and Amuquando regrets that the meaning of tourism 'is either taken for granted or pushed aside as unimportant in most perception studies in tourism' (2010: 35). He demonstrates how, in his study of residents' understandings of tourism in the lake Bosomtwe region of Ghana, a symbolic interactionist framework can show how people make sense of tourism in the context of their everyday lives.

We should also acknowledge that Blumer's critique of behaviourist social theory has been played out in the growing influence of interpretivism in the social sciences. In the tourism literature, this initially took the form of the adoption and defence of qualitative methodology (see, for example, Riley and Love, 2000). While Symbolic Interactionism was clearly influential in liberating social research from a behaviourist straightjacket, there are now 'multiple interpretive communities' each with its own criteria for evaluating interpretations' (Denzin and Lincoln, 2005: 26) and these are becoming more prominent in tourism research.

HISTORICAL DEVELOPMENT

The term Symbolic Interactionism was coined by Blumer (1969) who was in turn a student of G.H. Mead. It is premised on two assumptions. First, that people act toward things based on the meaning those things have for them and, second, these meanings are derived from social interaction and modified through interpretation.

These ideas capture a response within the Chicago School to the dominance of behaviourism and an emphasis on 'armchair' social theory in the sociology of the 1930s. Many empirical studies of urban life were conducted, first under the supervision of Mead and C.H. Cooley and then through a second generation of academics including Blumer, Goffman (classified as a symbolic interactionist but against his will), Thomas and Becker. The influential Grounded Theory emerged in the 1970s from the milieu of Symbolic Interactionism.

DESCRIPTION

As we have indicated above it was Blumer who progressed a distinct symbolic interactionist methodology. His notion of a sensitising concept and a commitment to naturalistic methodology stimulated interest in the use of qualitative methods. The adoption of participant observation and ethnographic methods enabled researchers to study social life in social settings. These earlier moves in social research have blossomed well beyond

Symbolic Interactionism by the 21st century. As Denzin and Lincoln comment in their introduction to the voluminous *SAGE Hanbook of Qualitative Research*, 'qualitative research is a situated activity that locates the observer in the world. It consists of a set of interpretive, material practices that make the world visible … qualitative researchers study things in their natural settings, attempting to make sense of or interpret phenomena in terms of the meanings people bring to them' (2005: 3). The legacy of Symbolic Interactionism is plainly visible in these authors' account of a wider contemporary move to embrace qualitative methods.

POTENTIAL CRITICISM

Social Interactionism has been criticised for over emphasising the social formation of the individual without taking into account structural constraints, such as age, class and gender. Its emphasis on the mundane day-to-day events of its subjects and the tendency to inflate, as Denzin and Lincoln (2005: 26) put it, 'the deviant into a sociological version of a screen hero' has also provided a point of critique. Gouldner's (1970) critique of Goffman's dramaturgy is perhaps the most sustained attack.

CROSS REFERENCES

Constructionism, Document Analysis, Ethnomethodology, Hermeneutics, Narrative, Phenomenology.

FURTHER READING

Generic

Blumer, H. (1954) What is wrong with social theory, *American Sociological Review*, 18: 3–10.
Blumer, H. (1969) *Symbolic Interactionism: Perspective and Method*. Berkeley, CA: University of California Press.
Denzin, N.K. and Lincoln, Y.S. (2005) *The SAGE Handbook of Qualitative Research*. London: Sage.
Gouldner, A. (1970) Other symptoms of the crisis: Goffman's dramaturgy and other new theories, in *The Coming Crisis of Western Sociology*. New York: Basic Books. pp. 378–90.

Tourism specific

Amuquando, F. (2010) Lay concepts of tourism in Bosomtwe basin, Ghana, *Annals of Tourism Research*, 37 (1): 34–51.

Brown, G.P. (1988) Observations on the use of symbolic interactionism in leisure, tourism and recreation, *Annals of Tourism Research*, 15 (4): 550–2.

Colton, C.W. (1987) Leisure, recreation, tourism: a symbolic interactionism view, *Annals of Tourism Research*, 14 (3): 345–60.

Colton, C.W. (1988) Additional symbolic interactionism view of LRT, *Annals of Tourism Research*, 15 (4): 552–4.

Haug, B., Dann. G. and Mehmetoglu, M. (2007) Little Norway in Spain: from tourism to migration, *Annals of Tourism Research*, 34 (1): 202–22.

Honggen Xiao (1997) Tourism and leisure in China: a tale of two cities, *Annals of Tourism Research*, 24 (2): 357–70.

Riley, W.R. and Love, L.L. (2000) The state of qualitative tourism research, *Annals of Tourism Research*, 27 (1): 164–87.

Ryan, C. and Gu, H. (2010) Constructionism and culture in research: understandings of the fourth Buddhist Festival, Wutaishan, China, *Tourism Management*, 31 (2): 167–78.

Visual Methods

Definition Research practices that generate and employ visual media and technologies as an integral part of a research project.

RELEVANCE

Research projects in tourism are wide open to the possibilities opened up by visual methods. Destination image and promotion is heavily dependent on the visual and the recording of holiday experiences has always incorporated visual dimensions from sketching and early photographic techniques, such as the Dagurreotype, to digital still and video camera technologies. There is, therefore, a rich stock of visual imagery to call upon. The origination of visual images through research is also possible and digital technologies are making manipulation, editing and storage of images an easier proposition for incorporation into theses and other research output formats.

APPLICATION

The application of visual methods in tourism research epitomises the turn to visual culture in the social sciences and we would argue there are few better topics than tourism to exemplify the dominance of the visual in social interactions at the turn of the 21st century. Knowles and Sweetman refer to the general trend as, ' ... a re-enchantment among social commentators with the texture of social life, the shifting and fragmented frameworks of knowledge in which we all operate and a determination to reach beyond words in producing accounts of the social world' (2004: 4).

As the following brief review of the literature demonstrates, tourism commentators in the academy have certainly embraced this opportunity, exemplified by the two volume set of studies published as readings in *Tourism and Visual Culture* (Burns et al., 2010a, 2010b). In Volume 1 the editors find that the dominant analytical themes reflected in the contributions to the book are of: nostalgia; the influence of photographic images over tourist perceptions; the sentimental associations of landscapes; the conception and use of space; and the negative consequences of the tourist gaze (Burns et al., 2010a). In the introduction to Volume 2 the editors identify four separate but interconnected methodological categories: semiotics/symbolism; visual sociology/photo-elicitation; image analysis for destinations and marketing; and visual ethnography (Burns et al., 2010b).

Researchers have utilised a wide variety of already existing images: film (Burns and Lester, 2005); television (Waade and Jorgensen, 2010); postage stamps (Raento, 2009); brochures (Hunter, 2008); and holiday snapshots (Botterill, 1989; Haldrup and Larsen, 2003). In many cases, researchers are interested in the symbolism or message of the image and they have variously produced accounts of national identity, capital cities, food and places, the family, and 'enduring' tourism destination imagery.

Fewer studies have been concerned with the production and distribution of pre-existing images. An exception is Rakic and Chambers' (2009) discussion of the production of moving images, in an analysis of Dziga Vertov's 1929 ground breaking film *The Man With the Movie Camera*, exploring the role of the film maker in visual ethnographic research. In another example of this genre, Feighery (2009) adopts Foucault's theoretical frame of power, surveillance and disciplinary regimes to show how 'stock' images of official tourism agencies 'script' tourism through a governing apparatus.

The majority of tourism research that utilises visual images has featured the production of the images by respondents. Visitor-employed photography has been adopted in destination image research (MacKay and Couldwell, 2006) and at tourist destinations for planning purposes (Garrod, 2007, 2008; Balomenou and Garrod, 2010). Images produced during the research process have also been used to explore social constructions of tourists' experiences. Hayllar et al. (2009) use visitor photographs to develop a phenomenological account of iconic buildings in Canberra, Australia. Cederholm (2004) analyses backpacker tourism and Caton and Santos (2008) utilise photographs taken by students studing abroad to examine the replication and reinforcement of media depictions in tourist's own photographic practices. The interplay between 'official' and tourist's own images is also played out in studies of the island of Bornholm (Larsen et al., 2006) and Venice (Parmeggiani, 2010).

An ethnographic approach to the use of visual methods is represented in a small number of studies. The tourist act of photographing at commemorative 'places that hurt' is explored by Sather-Wagstaff (2008), Rakic (2010) employs researcher created video in cultural tourism and Wharton et al. (2008) provides a photographic essay on the American South.

HISTORICAL DEVELOPMENT

The adoption of visual research methods is inextricably linked to technological developments in visual representation. Just as the growth in visual research in contemporary social science has been fuelled by the digitisation of images, so visual research of the face and body in medical science in the mid-19th century was boosted by the invention of photography in 1839. But technological developments alone cannot explain the fortunes of visual research methods. The climate of ideas about knowledge creation and production that surrounded any particular technological breakthrough has had equal influence over the value placed on the visual image in research practice. An example here might be the Polaroid Land camera, an invention in photography in 1948 that brought the processes of taking a photograph and viewing it within minutes together in the same piece of equipment. Such technological capacity would have lent itself very well to the recent growth in participant-created visual records of different experiences (including holidays) in social research but the prevailing conventions of what constituted social knowledge in the 1950s prevented its adoption as a research tool.

With the exception of social anthropology and human geography, and even here often questioned as politically suspect, 20th-century social science was dominated by the primacy of textual, tabular and statistical representations of knowledge. In sociology, for example, visual images disappeared from journals around the 1920s (Hamilton, 2006). The legitimacy of the visual is also entangled with divergent paradigms that, on the one hand, emphasise the documentary utility of the image and, on the other, concentrate on the symbolic aspects of image production and reading. The arguments here centre on the objectivity of the visual image. Challenges to objectification, in part, fuelled by the 'cultural turn' in sociology has emphasised the value of reading the symbolic texts of images. These debates on the value of the representation of the social world through images continue to reverberate around the contemporary use of visual research methods.

DESCRIPTION

Pink identifies four types of visual research:

1 Analysis of the content, process of production, or uses of existing visual images involving qualitative or quantitative content analysis.
2 Production of visual images as part of a research project to visually document activities and events, or in collaboration with informants to produce images that represent particular ideas, understandings, or worldviews.
3 Use of images in interviewing to elicit responses from informants.
4 Visual observations of events and activities. (2004: 1185)

She also points out that the use of images is nearly always in conjunction with other verbal or written methods of research and lists the output of visual research as including; photographs in written publications, photographic exhibitions or essays, ethnographic film and video, and interactive hypermedia projects using multiple media published in online, CD and DVD formats.

Banks provides a useful set of questions that he suggests all researchers could well ask of their data when using visual methods:

1   What is the image of? What is its content?
2   Who took it or made it, when and why?
3   How do other people come to have it, how do they read it, what do they do with it? (2001: 7)

POTENTIAL CRITICISM

We must return here to the arguments about the objective and subjective powers of the visual image. The objective claim presumed in the use of photography to develop a 'scientific' image type of mental patient or criminal in the later part of the 19th century has clearly been discredited but as we have seen in the discussion of visual research in the tourism literature the capturing of reality still underlies its use in tourism planning, for example.

CROSS REFERENCES

Document Analysis, Ethical Practice, Ethnomethodology, Hermeneutics, Phenomenology.

FURTHER READING

Generic

Banks, M. (2001) *Visual Methods in Social Research*. London: Sage.
Hamilton, P. (Ed.) (2006) *Visual Research Methods*, Vols 1–4. London: Sage.
Knowles, C. and Sweetman, P. (eds) (2004) *Picturing the Social Landscape: Visual Methods and the Sociological Imagination*. London: Routledge.
Pink, S. (2004) Visual research, in M. Lewis-Beck, R. Bryman and T.F. Liao (eds), *The SAGE Encyclopaedia of Social Science Research Methods*, Vol. 1. Thousand Oaks, CA: Sage. pp. 1185–6.

Tourism specific

Balomenou, N. and Garrod, B. (2010) Using volunteer-employed photography: seeing St David's peninsula through the eyes of locals and tourists, in P.M. Burns,

J.M. Lester and L. Bibbings (eds), *Tourism and Visual Culture, Volume 2: Methods and Cases*, Wallingford: CABI. pp. 111–19.

Botterill, D. (1989) Humanistic tourism? Personal constructions of a tourist: Sam visits Japan, *Leisure Studies*, 8: 281–93.

Burns, P. and Lester, J.A. (2005) Using visual evidence: the case of 'Cannibal Tours', in B.W. Ritchie, P. Burns and C. Palmer (eds), *Tourism Research Methods: Integrating Theory with Practice*, Wallingford: CABI. pp. 49–61.

Burns, P., Palmer, C. and Lester, J.A. (eds) (2010a) *Tourism and Visual Culture, Volume 1: Theories and Concepts*. Wallingford: CABI.

Burns, P., Palmer, C. and Lester, J.A. (eds) (2010b) *Tourism and Visual Culture, Volume 2: Methods and Cases*. Wallingford: CABI.

Caton, K. and Santos, C.A. (2008) Closing the hermeneutic circle? Photographic encounters with the other, *Annals of Tourism Research*, 35 (1): 7–26.

Cederholm, E.A. (2004) The use of photo-elicitation in tourism research – framing the backpacker experience, *Scandinavian Journal of Hospitality and Tourism*, 4 (3): 225–41.

Feighery, W. (2009) Tourism, stock photography and surveillance: a Foucauldian interpretation, *Journal of Tourism and Cultural Change*, 7 (3): 161–78.

Garrod, B. (2007) A snapshot into the past: the utility of volunteer-employed photography in planning and managing heritage tourism, *Journal of Heritage Tourism*, 2 (1): 14–35.

Garrod, B. (2008) Exploring place perception: a photo-based analysis, *Annals of Tourism Research*, 35 (2): 381–401.

Haldrup, M. and Larsen, J. (2003) The family gaze, *Tourist Studies*, 3 (1): 23–46.

Hayllar, B., Edwards, D., Griffin, T. and Dickson, T. (2009) Inside the triangle: images of a capital, in R. Maitland and B. Ritchie (eds), *City Tourism: National Capital Perspectives*. Wallingford: CABI. pp. 77–93.

Hunter, W.C. (2008) A typology of photographic representations for tourism: depictions of groomed spaces, *Tourism Management*, 29 (2): 354–65.

Larsen, J., Mykletun, R.J. and Haukeland, J.V. (2006) Picturing Bornholm: producing and consuming a tourist place through picturing practices, *Scandinavian Journal of Hospitality and Tourism*, 6 (2): 75–94.

MacKay, K.J. and Couldwell, C.M. (2006) Using visitor-employed photography to investigate destination image, *Journal of Travel Research*, 42 (4): 390–6.

Parmeggiani, P. (2010) Integrating multiple research methods: a visual sociology approach to Venice, in P.M. Burns, J.M. Lester and L. Bibbings (eds), *Tourism and Visual Culture, Volume 2: Methods and Cases*. Wallingford: CABI. pp. 94–110.

Raento, P. (2009) Tourism, nation, and the postage stamp: examples from Finland, *Annals of Tourism Research*, 36 (1): 124–48.

Rakic, T. (2010) Tales from the field: video and its potential for creating cultural tourism knowledge, in G. Richards and W. Munsters (eds), *Cultural Tourism Research Methods*. Wallingford: CABI. pp. 129–40.

Rakic, T. and Chambers, D. (2009) Researcher with a movie camera: visual ethnography in the field, *Current Issues in Tourism*, 12 (3): 271–90.

Sather-Wagstaff, J. (2008) Picturing experience, *Tourist Studies*, 8 (1): 77–103.

Waade, A.M. and Jorgensen, U.A. (2010) Haptic routes and digestive destinations in cooking series: images of food and place in 'Keith Floyd' and 'The Hairy Bikers' in relation to art history, *Journal of Tourism and Cultural Change*, 8 (1/2): 84–100.

Wharton, D., Megehee, C.M. and Spake, D.F. (2008) Southern attraction, southern attractions: a photographic essay, *International Journal of Culture, Tourism and Hospitality Research*, 2 (2): 102–14.

Index

index

key concepts in
tourism research